READING FOR TODAY INSIGHTS 2

FIFTH EDITION

LORRAINE C. SMITH
AND
NANCY NICI MARE

English Language Institute
Queens College
The City University of New York

Australia • Brazil • Mexico • Singapore • United Kingdom • United States

Reading for Today 2: Insights
Fifth Edition
Lorraine C. Smith and Nancy Nici Mare

Publisher: Sherrise Roehr

Executive Editor: Laura Le Dréan

Acquisitions Editor: Jennifer Monaghan

Senior Development Editor: Mary Whittemore

Editorial Assistant: Patricia Giunta

Director of Marketing: Ian Martin

Executive Marketing Manager: Ben Rivera

Product Marketing Manager: Dalia Bravo

Senior Director, Production: Michael Burggren

Content Production Manager: Mark Rzeszutek

Senior Print Buyer: Mary Beth Hennebury

Compositor: Lumina Datamatics, Inc.

Cover and Interior Design: Brenda Carmichael

Cover Photo: Ark Nova in Matsushima, Japan. Mobile, inflatable 500-seat concert hall designed by Arata Isozaki and Anish Kapoor. Photo courtesy of Lucerne Festival Ark Nova.

ISBN-13: 978-1-305-57997-2

National Geographic Learning
20 Channel Center Street
Boston, MA 02210
USA

Cengage Learning is a leading provider of customized learning solutions with office locations around the globe, including Singapore, the United Kingdom, Australia, Mexico, Brazil, and Japan. Locate your local office at **international.cengage.com/region**

Cengage Learning products are represented in Canada by Nelson Education, Ltd.

Visit National Geographic Learning online at **ngl.cengage.com**

Visit our corporate website at **www.cengage.com**

Printed in Canada
Print Number: 02 Print Year: 2016

CONTENTS

SCOPE & SEQUENCE

Unit & Theme	Chapter	Reading Skills	Vocabulary Skills	Critical Thinking Skills
UNIT 1 **Education in Today's World** Page 2	**CHAPTER 1** Work and College: You can do both! Page 4 A Different Kind of College Student 15	Previewing a reading Recalling information Scanning for information Skimming for main idea **Reading Skill Focus:** Using headings to create an outline	Understanding meaning from context **Word Forms:** Identifying parts of speech: nouns and verbs Understanding word connections	Creating a list Identifying reasons Developing ideas for the future Preparing a schedule Comparing schedules
	CHAPTER 2 A New Way to Apply to College Page 20 The Right College for You 28	Previewing a reading Recalling information Scanning for information **Reading Skill Focus:** Organizing information in a chart	Understanding meaning from context **Word Forms:** Recognizing the suffixes *-ion* and *-tion* Understanding content-specific vocabulary	Explaining opinions Comparing colleges Developing future plans Designing a nontraditional college Creating a video
UNIT 2 **Family Life** Page 32	**CHAPTER 3** How alike are identical twins? Page 34 Diary of a Father of Triplets 45	Previewing a reading Recalling information Scanning for information Skimming for main idea **Reading Skill Focus:** Understanding a bar graph	Understanding meaning from context **Word Forms:** Recognizing the suffix *-ness* Understanding antonyms	Categorizing information Describing personality traits Explaining opinions Assessing advantages and disadvantages Preparing interview questions Discussing questions related to the chapter topic
	CHAPTER 4 A Healthy Diet for You and Your Family Page 52 Why do I eat when I'm not hungry? 63	Previewing a reading Using a chart to answer questions Activating prior knowledge Scanning for information Skimming for main idea **Reading Skill Focus:** Creating a flowchart	Understanding meaning from context **Word Forms:** Recognizing the suffix *-ment* Understanding synonyms	Discussing reasons Creating and comparing lists Writing about personal experiences Planning a healthy diet Comparing diets Evaluating a menu Reporting on a restaurant meal

SCOPE & SEQUENCE

Unit & Theme	Chapter	Reading Skills	Vocabulary Skills	Critical Thinking Skills
UNIT 3 **Making a Difference** Page 70	**CHAPTER 5** Volunteer Vacations Page 72 Who volunteers? 82	Previewing a reading Using a diagram to answer questions Scanning for information Recalling information **Reading Skill Focus:** Organizing information in a chart	Understanding meaning from context **Word Forms:** Recognizing the suffix *-tion* Recognizing word connections	Evaluating volunteer organizations Explaining reasons Recording experiences Creating a list Preparing interview questions Discussing questions related to the chapter topic
	CHAPTER 6 Improving Lives with Pet Therapy Page 88 A New Way to Relieve Student Stress 99	Previewing a reading Scanning for information Recalling information **Reading Skill Focus:** Understanding a pie chart	Understanding meaning from context **Word Forms:** Recognizing the suffix *-ful* Prepositions that follow verbs	Describing pets Writing about relaxation techniques Choosing pets for people Writing about past experiences Analyzing information Assessing needs and costs
UNIT 4 **Technology Today and Tomorrow** Page 104	**CHAPTER 7** Robots: The Face of the Future Page 106 An Unusual Teacher 117	Previewing a reading Making a list to answer questions Predicting content Skimming for main idea **Reading Skill Focus:** Understanding a pie chart	Understanding meaning from context **Word Forms:** Recognizing the suffix *-ment* Recognizing connecting words	Predicting outcomes Considering advantages and disadvantages Illustrating a fictional robot Explaining opinions Designing an advertisement Creating and comparing lists
	CHAPTER 8 A blind man sees again! Page 122 A Bionic Hug 131	Previewing a reading Scanning for information Understanding types of questions Recalling information **Reading Skill Focus:** Understanding a graphic	Understanding meaning from context **Word Forms:** Recognizing the suffix *-ness* Understanding antonyms	Identifying types of technology Explaining opinions Writing about experiences Researching medical technology Creating and comparing lists

SCOPE & SEQUENCE

Unit & Theme	Chapter	Reading Skills	Vocabulary Skills	Critical Thinking Skills
UNIT 5 **International Scientists** Page 136	**CHAPTER 9** Alfred Nobel: A Man of Peace Page 138 Choosing Nobel Prize Winners 148	Previewing a reading Activating prior knowledge Scanning for information **Reading Skill Focus:** Creating a chart to summarize a reading	Understanding meaning from context **Word Forms:** Recognizing the suffixes *-ion* and *-ation* Recognizing the prefix *un–*	Preparing instructions Describing Nobel Prize nominees and winners Recording an autobiography Developing a fictional Nobel Prize category Evaluating Nobel Prize categories Researching past Nobel Prize winners
	CHAPTER 10 Marie Curie: Nobel Prize Winner Page 154 Irène Curie: Following in Her Mother's Footsteps 165	Previewing a reading Predicting content Scanning for information Skimming for main idea **Reading Skill Focus:** Understanding a timeline	Understanding meaning from context **Word Forms:** Recognizing the suffixes *-ance* and *-ence* Understanding synonyms	Examining reasons Preparing an autobiography or biography Describing experiences Predicting experiences Researching a historical figure Assessing discoveries
UNIT 6 **Earth's Resources and Dangers** Page 170	**CHAPTER 11** Oil as an Important World Resource Page 172 Fresh Water for the World 183	Previewing a reading Creating a list to answer questions Recording answers in a flowchart Scanning for information Skimming for main idea **Reading Skill Focus:** Understanding a bar graph	Understanding meaning from context **Word Forms:** Recognizing the suffix *-tion* Understanding synonyms	Considering advantages Describing scientific processes Evaluating scientific advances Inferring potential scenarios Creating and comparing lists Evaluating a process Researching energy types
	CHAPTER 12 Earthquakes: Powerful and Deadly Page 190 A Survivor's Story 200	Previewing a reading Scanning for information Recalling information **Reading Skill Focus:** Using an illustration and text to create a flowchart	Understanding meaning from context **Word Forms:** Recognizing the suffix *-ment* Understanding antonyms	Interviewing people Writing about experiences Developing a plan of action Describing an earthquake Labeling a map Analyzing statistics in a chart Creating a plan of action Researching natural disasters

PREFACE

Insights for Today, Fifth Edition, is a reading skills text intended for high-beginning English-as-a-second or foreign-language (ESL/EFL) students. The topics in this text are fresh and timely, and the book has a strong global focus.

Insights for Today is one in a series of five reading skills texts. The complete series, ***Reading for Today,*** has been designed to meet the needs of students from the beginning to the advanced levels and includes the following:

• *Reading for Today 1: Themes for Today*	beginning
• *Reading for Today 2: Insights for Today*	high-beginning
• *Reading for Today 3: Issues for Today*	intermediate
• *Reading for Today 4: Concepts for Today*	high-intermediate
• *Reading for Today 5: Topics for Today*	advanced

Insights for Today, Fifth Edition, provides students with essential practice in the types of reading skills they will need in an academic environment. It requires students not only to read text but also to extract basic information from various kinds of charts, graphs, illustrations, and photos. Beginning-level students are rarely exposed to this type of reading material. In addition, they are given the opportunity to speak and write about their own cultures and compare their experiences with those of students from other countries. The text includes real-life activities that give students tasks to complete outside the classroom. These tasks provide students with opportunities to practice reading, writing, speaking, and listening to English in the real world. Thus, all four skills are incorporated into each chapter.

Insights for Today, Fifth Edition, has been designed for flexible use by teachers and students. The text consists of six units. Each unit contains two chapters that deal with related topics. At the same time, though, each chapter is entirely separate in terms of content from the other chapter in that unit. This gives the instructor the option of either completing entire units or choosing individual chapters as the focus in class. Although the chapters are organized by level of difficulty, the teacher and students may choose to work with the chapters out of order, depending on available time and the interests of the class. The activities and exercises in each chapter have been organized to flow from general comprehension—including main ideas and supporting details—through vocabulary in context, to critical thinking skills. However, the teacher may choose to work on certain exercises in any order, depending on time and on the students' abilities.

The opening photos and the *Prereading* section before each reading help activate the students' background knowledge of the topic and encourage them to think about the ideas, facts, and vocabulary that will be presented in the reading passage. In fact, discussing photos in class helps lower-level students visualize what they are going to read about and gives them cues for the new vocabulary they will encounter. The exercises that follow the reading passage are intended to develop and improve reading proficiency, including the ability to learn new vocabulary from context and better comprehend English sentence structure. The activities also give students the opportunity to master useful vocabulary encountered in the reading passages through pair work and group discussions that lead them through comprehension of main ideas and specific information.

Lower-level language students need considerable visual reinforcement of ideas and vocabulary. Therefore, this text includes many photos and graphics that illustrate the ideas and concepts from the reading passages. In addition, many of the follow-up activities enable students to manipulate the information from the reading passages and other content from the chapter. In fact, the teacher may want the students to complete the charts and lists in the activities on the board.

Vocabulary is recycled throughout any given chapter. Experience has shown that low-level students especially need a lot of exposure to the same vocabulary and word forms. Repetition of vocabulary in varied contexts helps students not only understand the new vocabulary better, but also remember it.

A student-centered approach facilitates learning. Wherever possible, students should be actively engaged through pair work or small group work. Except during the actual process of reading, students should be actively engaged in almost all of the activities and exercises with a partner or in a small group. By working with others, students have more opportunities to interact in English. Student group work also allows the teacher to circulate in the classroom and give more individual attention to students than would be possible if the teacher were to direct the class work from the front of the room.

As students work through ***Insights for Today,*** they will learn and improve their reading skills and develop more confidence in their increasing proficiency in English. At the same time, teachers will be able to observe students' steady progress toward skillful, independent reading.

New to the Fifth Edition

The fifth edition of ***Insights for Today*** maintains the effective approach of the fourth edition with several significant improvements.

The fifth edition of ***Insights for Today*** incorporates a number of revisions and new material. Three completely new chapters have been added: *Work and College: You can do both!* and *A New Way to Apply to College* in Unit 1, and *A blind man sees again!* in Unit 4. In addition, the *Another Look* sections in Chapters 1, 2, 8, and 11 feature new readings. All other readings throughout the text have been updated as well. The first exercise in the *Vocabulary Skills* section, *Recognizing Word Forms,* has been revised to put the items in the context of the reading, making a clearer connection between the reading passage and the exercise. A second exercise has been added to this section that focuses on various vocabulary skills, including antonyms, synonyms, and sentence connectors. A new *Reading Skill* section focuses on a specific reading skill, for example, understanding graphs and charts, and creating flowcharts and timelines. Also new to the fifth edition is a *Critical Thinking* section. The activities in this section encourage students to use the information and vocabulary from the reading passage both orally and in writing, and to think beyond the reading passage and form their own opinions. In addition, the fifth edition includes new photos, graphs, and charts, all of which are designed to enhance students' comprehension of the readings.

These enhancements to ***Insights for Today, Fifth Edition,*** have been made to help students improve their reading skills, to reinforce vocabulary, and to encourage interest in the topics. These skills are intended to prepare students for academic work and the technical world of information they will soon encounter.

INTRODUCTION

How to Use This Book

Every chapter in this book consists of the following sections:

- *Prereading*
- *Reading Passage*
- *Fact Finding*
- *Reading Analysis*
- *Vocabulary Skills*
- *Vocabulary in Context*
- *Reading Skill*
- *Another Look*
- *Topics for Discussion and Writing*
- *Critical Thinking*
- *Crossword Puzzle*

The format of each chapter in the book is consistent. Although each chapter can be done entirely in class, some exercises may be assigned for homework. This, of course, depends on the individual teacher's preference as well as the availability of class time. Each chapter consists of the following sections.

Prereading

The *Prereading* activity is designed to activate students' background knowledge, stimulate their interest, and provide preliminary vocabulary for the passage itself. The importance of prereading activities should not be underestimated. Studies have shown the positive effects of prereading in motivating students and in enhancing reading comprehension. In fact, prereading discussion of topics and visuals has been shown to be very effective in improving reading comprehension. Students need to spend time describing and discussing the photos and the prereading questions. Furthermore, students should try to relate the topic to their own experience and try to predict what they are going to read about. The teacher can facilitate the students' discussions by writing their guesses and predictions about the reading on the board. This procedure helps motivate students by providing a reason for reading. This process also helps the teacher evaluate the students' knowledge of the content they are about to read in order to provide any necessary background information. After they have read the passage, students can check their predictions for accuracy. The important point to keep in mind is not whether the students' guesses are correct, but rather that they think about the reading beforehand and formulate predictions about the text. Once students have considered the title, the accompanying photos, and the prereading questions, they are ready to read the passage.

The Reading Passage

As students read the passage for the first time, they should be encouraged to pay attention to the main ideas and important details. After students read the passage to themselves, the teacher may want to read the passage aloud to them. At lower levels, students are very eager to learn pronunciation and feel that this practice is helpful to them. Moreover, reading aloud provides students with an appropriate model for pronunciation and intonation, and it helps them hear how words are grouped together by meaning. Students can also listen to the readings on the audio CD.

Students may wish to maintain individual records of their reading rate. They can keep track of the time it takes them to read a passage for the first time and then record the length of time it takes them to read it a second time. Students should be encouraged to read a text from beginning to end without stopping and to read at a steady pace, grouping words and phrases in meaningful chunks. Once they have established a base time for reading, they can work to improve their reading rate as they progress through the book.

Fact Finding

After the first reading, students will have a general idea of the information in the passage. The purpose of the *Fact Finding* exercises is to check students' general comprehension. Students will read the *True/False* statements and check whether the information is true or false. If the statement is false, the students will go back to the passage and find the line(s) that contain the correct information. They will then rewrite the statement so that it is true. This activity can be done individually or in pairs. Doing this exercise in pairs allows students to discuss their answers with their partner and to explain their reasons for deciding if a statement is true or false. When all the students have finished the exercise, they can report their answers to the class.

Reading Analysis

At this point, students have read the passage at least two times, and they should be familiar with the main idea and the content of the reading. The *Reading Analysis* exercise gives students an opportunity to learn new vocabulary from context. In this exercise, students read questions and answer them. This exercise requires students to think about the meanings of words and phrases, the structure of sentences and paragraphs, and the relationships of ideas to each other. This exercise is very effective when done in pairs or in groups. Students can also work individually, but working together provides an excellent opportunity for students to discuss possible answers.

Vocabulary Skills

This section consists of two parts. The first part focuses on recognizing word forms.

As an introduction to this exercise, it is recommended that teachers first review parts of speech, especially verbs, nouns, adjectives, and adverbs. Teachers should point out the position of each word form in a sentence. Students will develop a sense for which part of speech is missing in a given sentence. Teachers should also point out clues to tense and number, and whether an idea is affirmative or negative. Each section has its own instructions, depending on the particular pattern that is being introduced. For example, in the section containing words that take *-tion* in the noun form, teachers can explain that students will look at the verb and noun forms of these words in the exercise. Teachers can use the examples in the directions for each chapter's *Recognizing Word Forms* section to see that the students understand the exercise. All of the sentences in this exercise are content specific, which helps not only reinforce the vocabulary, but also check the students' comprehension of the passage. This activity is very effective when done in pairs because students can discuss their answers. After students have a working knowledge of this type of exercise, it can be assigned for homework. The focus of Part 2 of the *Vocabulary Skills* section varies. The purpose of this section is to provide students with a range of ways to learn and practice new vocabulary, and to make logical connections by working with words that are commonly paired or that are related to a particular topic. The exercises in this section focus on a variety of important vocabulary-related topics, including antonyms, synonyms, sentence connectors, common collocations, topic-specific vocabulary, and prefixes.

Vocabulary in Context

This is a fill-in exercise designed as a review of the vocabulary items covered in the *Reading Analysis* and/or *Recognizing Word Forms* exercises. In this exercise, the target words are used in new sentences, giving the students the opportunity to practice the new vocabulary. It can be assigned for homework as a review or done in class as group work.

Reading Skill

Each chapter includes a new *Reading Skill* section, which provides instruction and practice with a specific reading skill, such as understanding pie charts, line graphs, bar graphs, or timelines. Students are also asked to create a flowchart or an outline.

This section is very effective when done in pairs or small groups. The exercises in these sections may also be done individually, but group work gives the students an opportunity to discuss their work.

Another Look

The second reading in each chapter provides another point of view or additional information related to the main reading. Students should focus on improving general comprehension, relating this reading to the primary reading, and considering the ideas and information as they engage in the *Topics for Discussion and Writing* and *Critical Thinking* activities. It is not necessary to spend additional time on unfamiliar vocabulary unless it interferes with students' ability to respond to the questions.

Topics for Discussion and Writing

This section provides ideas or questions for students to think about and work on alone, in pairs, or in small groups. Students are encouraged to use the information and vocabulary from the passages both orally and in their writing. The writing assignments may be done entirely in class, started in class and finished at home, or done entirely for homework. The last activity in this section is a journal-writing assignment that provides students with an opportunity to reflect on the topic of the chapter and respond to it in some personal way. Students should be encouraged to keep a journal and to write in it regularly. The students' journal writing may be purely personal, or students may choose to have the teacher read their entries. If the teacher reads the entries, the journals should be considered a free writing activity and should be responded to rather than corrected.

Critical Thinking

This section contains various activities appropriate to the information in the passages. Some activities are designed for pair and small group work. Students are encouraged to use the information and vocabulary from the passages both orally and in writing. The critical thinking questions and activities provide students with an opportunity to think about some aspect of the chapter topic and to share their own thoughts and opinions about it. The goal of this section is for students to go beyond the reading itself and to form their own ideas and opinions on aspects of the topic. Teachers may also use these questions and activities as homework or in-class assignments. The activities in the *Critical Thinking* sections help students interact with the real world as many exercises require students to go outside the classroom to collect specific information.

Crossword Puzzle

The *Crossword Puzzle* in each chapter is based on the vocabulary used in that chapter. Students can go over the puzzle orally if pronunciation practice with letters is needed. Teachers can have the students spell out their answers in addition to pronouncing the words themselves. Students invariably enjoy doing crossword puzzles. They are a fun way to reinforce the vocabulary presented in the various exercises in each chapter. Crossword puzzles also require students to pay attention to correct spelling. At the same time, students need to connect the meaning of a word and think about the word itself. If the teacher prefers, students can do the *Crossword Puzzle* on their own or with a partner in their free time, or after they have completed an in-class assignment and are waiting for the rest of their classmates to finish.

Index of Key Words and Phrases

The Index of Key Words and Phrases is at the back of the book. This section contains a list of words and phrases from all of the reading passages in the chapters for easy reference. The *Index of Key Words and Phrases* may be useful to students to help them locate words they need or wish to review. The words that are part of the Academic Word List are indicated with an icon.

Skills Index

The *Skills Index* lists the different skills presented and/or practiced in the book.

ACKNOWLEDGMENTS

The authors and publisher would like to thank the following reviewers:

Sola Armanious, Hudson County Community College; **Marina Broeder**, Mission College; **Kara Chambers**, Mission College; **Peter Chin**, Waseda University International; **Feri Collins**, BIR Training Center; **Courtney DeRouen**, University of Washington; **Jeanne de Simon**, University of West Florida; **Shoshana Dworkin**, BIR Training Center; **Cindy Etter**, University of Washington International and English Language Programs; **Ken Fackler**, University of Tennessee at Martin; **Jan Hinson**, Carson Newman University; **Chigusa Katoku**, Mission College; **Sharon Kruzic**, Mission College; **Carmella Lieskle**, Shimane University; **Yelena Malchenko**, BIR Training Center; **Mercedes Mont**, Miami Dade College; **Ewa Paluch**, BIR Training Center; **Barbara Pijan**, Portland State University, Intensive English Language Program; **Julaine Rosner**, Mission College; **Julie Scales**, University of Washington; **Mike Sfiropoulos**, Palm Beach State College; **Barbara Smith-Palinkas**, Hillsborough Community College; **Eileen Sotak**, BIR Training Center; **Matthew Watterson**, Hongik University; **Tristinn Williams**, IELP—University of Washington; **Iryna Zhylina**, Hudson County Community College; **Ana Zuljevic**, BIR Training Center

From the Authors:
We are thankful to everyone at Cengage, especially Laura LeDréan, Mary Whittemore, Patricia Giunta, and Jennifer Monaghan, for their unwavering support. We are extremely grateful to all the teachers and students who use our book and who never hesitate to give us such incredible feedback. As always, we are very appreciative of the ongoing encouragement from our families, friends, and colleagues.

Dedication:
To Steven

L.C.S. and N.N.M.

UNIT **1**

Education in Today's World

North Carolina State University students working in the Hunt Library

1. Is it a good idea to have a job when you are in school? Why or why not?
2. Is it easy to apply to college in your country? Why or why not?

CHAPTER 1 Work and College: You can do both!

Prereading

1. Look at the photo. This person is
   a. a waiter.
   b. a student.
   c. a student and a waiter.

2. Look at the title of the chapter. In the United States, many college students go to school and have jobs, too. What kind of jobs do they have? Make a list and write your ideas in the chart on page 5. Share it with your classmates.

Jobs for College Students

Reading

CD 1
TR 2

Read the following passage carefully. Then complete the exercises that follow.

College and Work: You can do both!

Everyone knows that a college student's life isn't easy. Most students take four or five classes each semester. Students must study, do homework, and take tests for every class. They have very busy schedules. But for some students, their schedules can be even more difficult. In the United States, 80 percent of all college students work either part-time or full-time while they are in college. In other words, many students go to college and have a job at the same time.

Balance School and Work

Jobs can be important for college students. Of course, students earn money, but jobs can teach students other things, too. Students can get a lot of experience from their jobs. Students who work can also learn how to spend and save their money carefully. This experience can help them after they graduate from college. However, they also need to learn to balance school and work at the same time. Here are some suggestions that may help.

Find an Understanding Employer

Be sure to tell your employer that you are a college student. Sometimes you might need to leave work early to prepare for a class. Sometimes you might need to take time off to study for an exam. A good boss will understand your situation.

Schedule Your Time Carefully

Make a schedule of your classes and give yourself enough time to study. Plan your work hours carefully. Your classes are most important right now. Too much work can make you very tired. It's hard to do classwork when you feel this way.

Don't Work Too Many Hours

Perhaps you have classes for 12–18 hours per week. This might not sound like a lot of hours. However, you also need time to study and do homework. Because of this, college students cannot work more than 20 hours per week and still do their schoolwork well.

Work Weekends

Weekends are a good time to work. You will have more time to study and prepare for your classes on weekdays.

Make Time for Fun

A busy college student needs time to relax, too. Take breaks occasionally and schedule some time each week to relax and have fun. Go out with friends and enjoy yourself. Then you will feel ready to go back to your classes and your job, too!

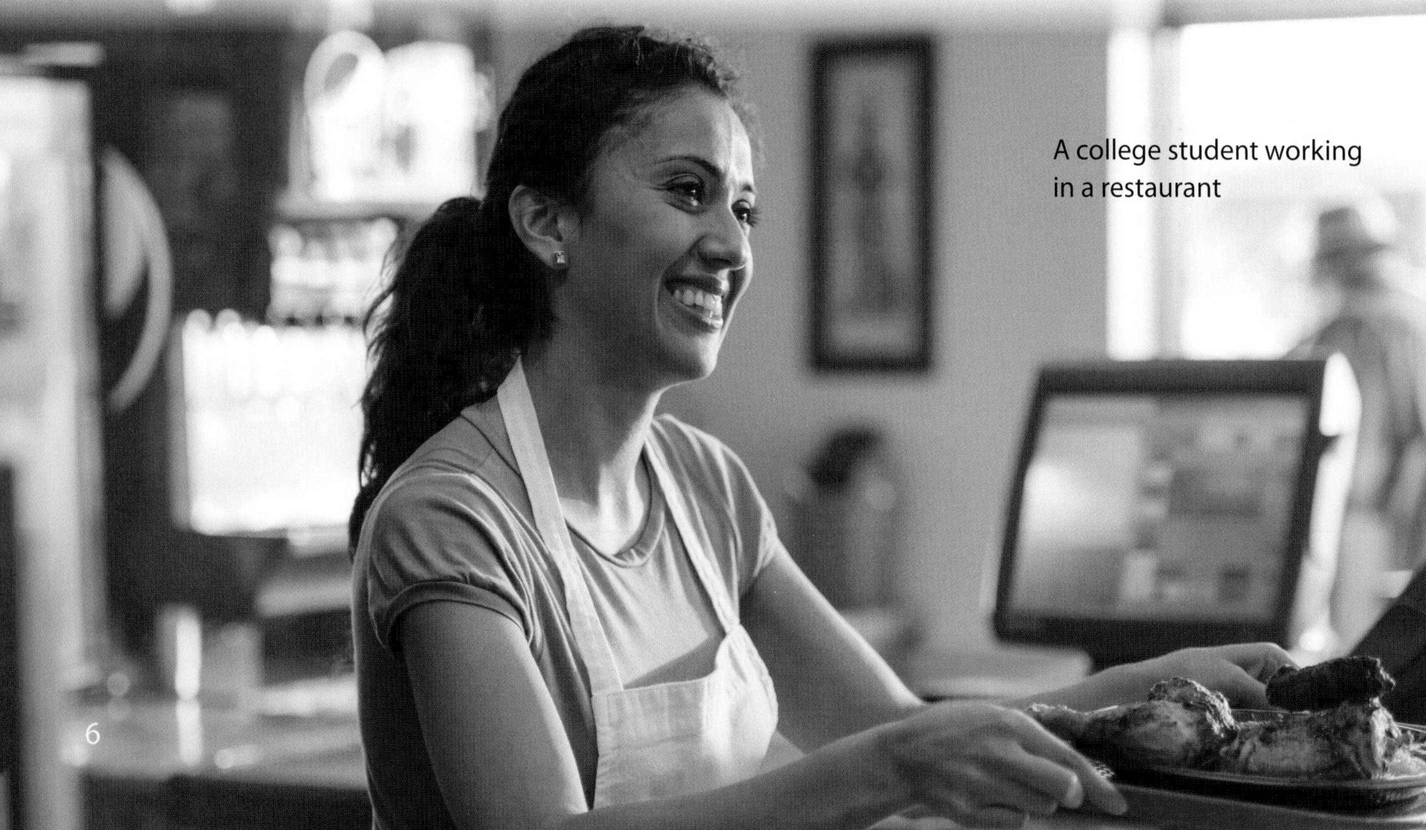

A college student working in a restaurant

Fact Finding

Read the passage again. Then read the following statements. Check (√) whether each statement is True or False. If a statement is false, rewrite it so that it is true. Then go back to the passage and find the line that supports your answer.

1. _____ True _____ False In the United States, most college students have jobs.

   ____

2. _____ True _____ False Students learn how to spend and save money carefully from their teachers.

   ____

3. _____ True _____ False A good boss will help you study for your classes.

   ____

4. _____ True _____ False Students' jobs are most important in college.

   ____

5. _____ True _____ False It's a good idea for students to work on weekends.

   ____

Reading Analysis

Read each question carefully. Circle the letter or the number of the correct answer.

1. In the United States, 80 percent of all college students work either part-time or full-time. **In other words**, many students go to college and have a job at the same time.

   The sentence after **in other words** tells you

   a. new information.

   b. the same information.

   c. different information.

2. Jobs can be important for college students. **Of course**, students earn money.

Of course means

a. also.
b. but.
c. surely.

3. Students can get a lot of **experience** from their jobs. This experience can help them after they **graduate**.

a. **Experience** means
   1. money.
   2. help.
   3. knowledge.

b. **Graduate** means
   1. start college.
   2. finish college.
   3. get a new job.

4. **Students need to learn to balance school and work at the same time.**

This sentence means students must

a. make enough time for work and school.
b. make more time for classes.
c. work more hours.

5. Here are some **suggestions** that may help.

Suggestions are

a. words.
b. ideas.
c. places.

6. Sometimes you might need to take time off to study for an exam. A good **boss** will understand your **situation**.

a. This means that
   1. you can take time off.
   2. you can't take time off.

b. **Situation** means
   1. position.
   2. unhappiness.
   3. problem.

c. **Boss** means
   1. classmate.
   2. teacher.
   3. employer.

7. Make a **schedule** of your classes.
A **schedule** is

a. the names of the classes.
b. the days and times you do things.
c. a list of the things you do.

8. **Plan** your work hours carefully.
Plan means

a. write.
b. organize.
c. understand.

9. **Perhaps** you have classes for 12–18 hours **per week**.

a. **Perhaps** means
   1. however.
   2. maybe.
   3. sometimes.
b. **Per week** means
   1. each week.
   2. one week only.
   3. one week each month.

10. **Weekends** are a good time to work. You will have more time to study and prepare for classes on **weekdays**.

a. **Weekends** are
   1. Saturday and Sunday.
   2. Monday, Tuesday, Wednesday, Thursday, and Friday.
b. **Weekdays** are
   1. Saturday and Sunday.
   2. Monday, Tuesday, Wednesday, Thursday, and Friday.

11. A busy college student needs time to **relax**, too.
Relax means

a. do homework.
b. rest and enjoy yourself.
c. don't do homework.

12. **Take a break** means

a. stop school.
b. stop your job and get another job.
c. take time away from what you are doing.

13. What is the main idea of this reading passage?

a. It's not easy to work and go to school at the same time.
b. Most college students in the United States have jobs.
c. It's important to balance work and school carefully.

Vocabulary Skills

PART 1

Recognizing Word Forms

In English, the noun form and the verb form of some words are the same, for example, *walk (v.)*, *walk (n.)*.

Read each sentence. Complete each sentence with the correct word form on the left. Then circle *(v.)* if you are using a verb or *(n.)* if you are using a noun. Write all the verbs in the simple present. The nouns may be singular or plural.

schedule **1.** Students ________________ their work hours carefully. Their
(v.) / (n.)

________________ include their jobs and their classes.
(v.) / (n.)

balance **2.** It's important to have a good ________________
(v.) / (n.)

between school and work. Some students ________________
(v.) / (n.)

their time by working during the day and taking classes in the evening.

experience **3.** Students ________________ many new things when they get
(v.) / (n.)

jobs. These new ________________ can be very helpful after
(v.) / (n.)

they graduate from college.

work **4.** Some students ________________ on the weekends. Then they do
(v.) / (n.)

their ________________ for school on weekdays.
(v.) / (n.)

plan **5.** Students often make ________________ with their friends.
(v.) / (n.)

They ________________ to go out and relax.
(v.) / (n.)

PART 2

Understanding Word Connections

Word connections are important. They can help you when you write and speak. For example, the verb *take* connects with many nouns: *take a class, take a test, take an exam, take time, take a break, take a minute.*

Read the following sentences. Choose the correct word for each sentence. Fill in the blanks.

break	class	minute	test	time

1. Can you take a ________________ to help me with my homework? I only need a little help.

2. We have to take a grammar ________________ next week. Let's study together.

3. Before you start the test, take some ________________ to read all the questions.

4. I always take a ________________ for about five minutes every hour when I am studying for a test.

5. John needs to take a ________________ in biology before he can graduate.

Vocabulary in Context

Read the following sentences. Complete each sentence with the correct word or phrase from the box. Use each word or phrase only once.

employer *(n.)*	of course	relax *(v.)*	suggestions *(n.)*
experience *(n.)*	plans *(v.)*	schedule *(n.)*	weekend *(n.)*

1. Clara has a very busy ________. She works full-time and takes classes, too.
2. I need to find a job, but I don't know where to look. Do you have any ________?
3. College is a good ________ for students. They learn a lot and meet new people, too.
4. Carlos is taking six classes this semester. ________, he has a lot of homework!
5. Austin is a waiter. His ________ owns the restaurant where he works.
6. Lena ________ to meet her classmates after school. Then they can study together.
7. After I finish my homework, I ________ and play computer games.
8. Daniel works every evening. He does all his schoolwork on the ________.

Reading Skill

Using Headings to Create an Outline

Readings often have headings. Headings introduce new ideas in the reading, so it is important to notice them when you read. Also, using headings to create an outline can help you understand and remember what you read.

Read the passage again. Use the sentences below to complete the outline.

- Plan your work hours carefully.
- You also need time to study and do homework.
- Students can get a lot of experience from their jobs.
- Go out with friends and enjoy yourself.
- Tell your employer that you are a college student.
- You will have more time to study and prepare for your classes on weekdays.
- Most students take four or five classes each semester.

I. Introduction: A College Student's Life Isn't Easy.

A.

B. Students must study, do homework, and take tests for every class.

C. In the United States, 80 percent of all college students work part-time or full-time while they are in college.

II. Balance School and Work

A. Students earn money.

B.

C. Students who work learn how to spend and save their money carefully.

III. Find an Understanding Employer

A.

B. Sometimes you might need to leave work early to prepare for a class or to study.

C. A good boss will understand your situation.

IV. Schedule Your Time Carefully

A. Make a schedule of your classes and give yourself enough time to study.

B.

V. Don't Work Too Many Hours

A.

B. Most college students cannot work more than 20 hours per week.

VI. Work Weekends

A.

VII. Make Time for Fun

A. A busy college student needs time to relax, too.

B.

Another Look

CD 1 TR 3

Read the following passage about a different kind of college student. Then answer the questions that follow.

A Different Kind of College Student

On most college campuses, the students are similar. They go to college right after they finish high school, so they are about the same age. Many have very little experience in the real world. But some college students are different. Some may be older, have full-time jobs, or have children, too. Hope Long is different. She is a student at Angelo State University. However, Hope is much older than her classmates because she was in the U.S. Marine Corps for 20 years before she went to college.

"I joined the Marine Corps to become a Russian linguist," says Hope. "My dream was always to learn many different languages." After the Marine Corps, Hope was ready to go to college to follow her dream. Now she is studying English, French, and Spanish. Hope is not a traditional student. She is retired now, so she does not have to work. As a result, she has time to follow her dream.

Right now Hope is planning her schedule for next year. She wants to take Russian and German classes. Hope tells other students to never give up on their dreams. Dreams may take a lot of time, but one day they can come true.

Nontraditional students work together on an assignment.

QUESTIONS FOR ANOTHER LOOK

1. Why are most college students similar? Check (√) all that apply.

a. _____ They are usually the same age.
b. _____ They study English.
c. _____ They all go to the same school.
d. _____ They go to college after they finish high school.
e. _____ They don't have a lot of experience in the real world.

2. Why is Hope Long different? Check (√) all that apply.

a. _____ She went to college after high school.
b. _____ She was in the Marine Corps before she went to college.
c. _____ She has a full-time job.
d. _____ She is retired.
e. _____ She is older than most college students.

3. What is Hope Long's dream?

____

4. Hope Long has time to follow her dream now because

a. she doesn't have a family.
b. she doesn't have to work.
c. she is older than her classmates.

Topics for Discussion and Writing

1. Do you think it's a good idea to have a job in college? Why or why not?

2. In your country, do college students usually have jobs? What kinds of jobs do they have?

3. Hope Long is not a traditional student because she was in the Marine Corps for 20 years before she went to college. What other students are not traditional students?

4. Write in your journal. What are your dreams for the future?

Critical Thinking

1. What school schedule is good for you? Do you want to have a job in college? Make a college schedule. Include time for a part-time job. Make sure you have enough time to relax, too. Compare your schedule with your classmates' schedules.

Sunday	Monday	Tuesday	Wednesday	Thursday	Friday	Saturday

2. Discuss this question with a partner: In the United States, 80 percent of college students have jobs. What do you think are some reasons for this?

Crossword Puzzle

Review the words in the box below. Then read the clues on the next page. Write the words in the correct spaces in the puzzle.

balance	experience	plan	suggestion
boss	graduate	relax	weekdays
break	per	schedule	weekend
employer	perhaps	situation	

Crossword Puzzle Clues

ACROSS CLUES

2. In the winter, we take a __________ from classes for several weeks.

5. Monday, Tuesday, Wednesday, Thursday, and Friday are __________.

8. We like to __________ for a few hours before we do our homework.

11. Susan has a __________ to travel for a month after she finishes college.

13. You are in a difficult __________ if you cannot take time off work to study.

14. If you are tired, __________ you need to rest for a while.

15. John works three days __________ week. He is part-time.

DOWN CLUES

1. We will __________ from college in three years.

3. Your __________ is the person you work for.

4. Saturday and Sunday are __________ days.

6. I have a very good __________ for you. Why don't you take an extra class during the summer?

7. Maria has five years of __________ as a secretary.

9. I have a good __________ between work and school.

10. I have a very busy __________ because I go to class during the day and work every evening.

12. My manager is a good __________. She lets me leave work early three days a week.

CHAPTER 2 A New Way to Apply to College

Prereading

1. Look at the photo. What is this person doing?
   a. Taking a picture
   b. Making a video
   c. Watching a movie

2. Look at the title of this chapter. Why is this person doing this?
   a. He needs a new job.
   b. He likes to go to the movies.
   c. He wants to go to college.

Goucher College campus allows students to submit a two-minute video application.

Reading

CD 1
TR 4

Read the following passage carefully. Then complete the exercises that follow.

A New Way to Apply to College

In the United States, high school students take tests to apply for college. American students must take the SAT.[1] Students from other countries take the TOEFL.[2] In addition, all students must complete long, complicated application forms. This is the traditional way to apply for college. However, one college has a new way to do it. Students do not need to take any tests to apply to Goucher College in Towson, Maryland. Instead, Goucher College accepts video applications.

Students make a short, two-minute video of themselves to apply to Goucher. José Bowen is the president of the college. He believes that college applications can be very stressful. Most high school students have cell phones, and they know how to make videos very easily. President Bowen says, "At Goucher College, we want students to tell us who they really are. All students are different. Some are scientists, artists, or athletes. We want to attract different kinds of students to our college."

[1] The **SAT** is a college admission test that shows your knowledge of reading, writing, and math—subjects that high school students learn.

[2] The **TOEFL** test shows that you can use and understand English at the university level.

Of course, students who apply to Goucher College can send a traditional application, transcripts, and letters of recommendation from their teachers. A transcript is an official record of your grades from your school. A teacher or an employer usually writes a letter of recommendation to give some information about an applicant. For example, a letter of recommendation may say that the applicant is an excellent student or is very responsible. But President Bowen believes that a long application and recommendations do not always show a student's abilities. The video application has a big advantage. It gives students another way to enter the college. Students make a video that answers this question: How do you see yourself at Goucher? In addition, they send two of their high school assignments. For example, the assignments can be an essay, a science report, or a piece of artwork. "We want to make it possible for more students to apply," Bowen says. "It's much simpler to make a video than to write an essay or fill out a long application."

A video application can also be an advantage for students who have low grades. Carrie is a freshman at Goucher College. She used a video to apply to the school. "I was always a good student in high school, but I didn't get good grades. Whenever I took a test, I got very nervous. I was afraid to take the SAT," says Carrie. "I was afraid to get a low score." Carrie made the choice to send in a video application. Goucher College accepted her. Now Carrie is a successful college student. She says, "I always wanted to go to college, so I'm very happy to be here. The video application was the way for me to begin my college education."

Fact Finding

Read the passage again. Then read the following statements. Check (√) whether each statement is True or False. If a statement is false, rewrite the statement so that it is true. Then go back to the passage and find the line that supports your answer.

1. _____ True _____ False All students must take the SAT to apply for college.

____

2. _____ True _____ False College application forms are long and difficult.

____

3. _____ True _____ False You can use a video application for all U.S. colleges.

____

4. ____ True ____ False Letters of recommendation usually come from family members.

____

5. ____ True ____ False Students can use a traditional application to apply to Goucher College.

____

6. ____ True ____ False Students sometimes get low scores on tests because they are nervous.

____

Reading Analysis

Read each question carefully. Circle the letter or the number of the correct answer, or write the answer in the space provided.

1. a. What is the SAT?

____

b. How do you know this?

____

c. This information is called
1. an example.
2. a definition.
3. a footnote.

2. **In addition**, all students must complete long, **complicated** application forms.

a. **In addition** means
1. but.
2. first.
3. also.

b. **Complicated** means
1. easy.
2. difficult.
3. careful.

3. This is the **traditional** way to apply to college.

What is the **traditional** way to apply to college?

a. Students send a video application.
b. Students take a test and write a long application.
c. Students finish high school first.

4. José Bowen believes that college applications can be very **stressful**. Something **stressful** makes you feel
   a. upset.
   b. tired.
   c. busy.

5. "We want to **attract** different kinds of students to our college." **Attract** means
   a. look for.
   b. bring.
   c. find.

6. A **transcript** is an **official** record of your grades from your school.
   a. A **transcript** is
      1. a list of the classes you took and the grades you received.
      2. a record of the schools you attended.
      3. a list of the teachers who taught your classes.
   b. An **official** record
      1. comes from you.
      2. comes from a school or business.
      3. comes from a teacher.

7. What is a **letter of recommendation**?
   a. A letter from a teacher that gives information about the student
   b. A letter from a student that gives information about the college
   c. A long, complicated application form

8. The video application has a big **advantage**.
   An **advantage** is something that is
   a. easy.
   b. helpful.
   c. new.

9. It's much **simpler** to make a video than to write an essay or **fill out** a long application.
   a. **Simpler** means
      1. harder.
      2. easier.
      3. better.
   b. **Fill out** a long application means
      1. finish an application.
      2. start an application.
      3. write an application.

10. Carrie Long is a **freshman** at Goucher College.
A **freshman** is

a. a new student.
b. a first-year student.
c. a high school student.

11. What is the main idea of this reading?

a. Students can use a video application to apply to some colleges in the United States.
b. American students take the SAT to apply to college.
c. Traditional college applications are very complicated.

Vocabulary Skills

PART 1

Recognizing Word Forms

In English, some verbs become nouns by adding *-ion* or *-tion*, for example, *educate (v.), education (n.).*

Read each sentence. Complete each sentence with the correct word form on the left. Write all the verbs in the simple present. The nouns may be singular or plural.

correct ***(v.)***	**1.** Teachers always __________ students' essays. These
correction ***(n.)***	__________ can be very helpful to the students.
apply ***(v.)***	**2.** Carrie sent a video __________ to Goucher College. However,
application ***(n.)***	most students __________ to colleges in the traditional way.
recommend ***(v.)***	**3.** Teachers often __________ colleges that are good for their students.
recommendation ***(n.)***	These __________ help students decide where to go.
attract ***(v.)***	**4.** Video applications __________ many different kinds of students.
attraction ***(n.)***	President Bowen thinks this __________ is good for Goucher College.
inform ***(v.)***	**5.** Students can get a lot of __________ online about colleges and
information ***(n.)***	universities. Teachers also __________ students about them.

PART 2

Understanding Content-Specific Vocabulary

We use special vocabulary for a specific subject or activity. For example, we use the words in the box below for college applications.

Match each word, phrase, or abbreviation with its definition. Write your answers in the spaces provided.

application form	letter of recommendation	TOEFL	video application
assignment	SAT	transcript	

1. ____________________ : a test that shows you can understand and use English at a university level
2. ____________________ : a way to apply for college by making a film of yourself
3. ____________________ : an official record of courses you took and grades you received
4. ____________________ : a teacher or employer writes this to show you are a good student or a good worker
5. ____________________ : something that you fill in with important information to apply to college
6. ____________________ : a specific amount of work your teacher asks you to do, usually for homework
7. ____________________ : a test American students take for college admission

Vocabulary in Context

Read the following sentences. Complete each sentence with the correct word or phrase from the box. Use each word or phrase only once.

advantage *(n.)*	assignments *(n.)*	in addition	stressful *(adj.)*
apply *(v.)*	essay *(n.)*	simple *(adj.)*	successful *(adj.)*

1. It's very ____________________ to get to my school. I only need to take one bus.
2. The students wrote an ____________________ about their countries in class.

3. The teacher gave us a lot of homework, so I have a lot of ____________________ to do tonight.

4. Many students study hard and have jobs, too. This can be very ____________________ for them.

5. Next semester, Lynn will study biology and Spanish. ____________________, she will study math and psychology.

6. I don't need a car because there are many buses and trains near my apartment. This is an ____________________ of living in a big city.

7. Simon studies hard and goes to class every day. He wants to be a ____________________ student.

8. In the United States, many students ____________________ for college before they finish high school.

Reading Skill

Organizing Information in a Chart

It's important to be able to create charts. Charts can help you organize and understand information that you read.

Read the passage again. Use the information in the story to complete the chart below.

	Traditional College Application	Video Application
What types of student is each application good for?		
How do students do this?		

Another Look

CD 1 TR 5 **Read the following passage about different kinds of colleges. Then answer the questions that follow.**

The Right College for You

Most college students take about five classes—or 15 credits—each semester. They usually go to classes on the same college campus for four years. This is the traditional college experience. However, many colleges in the United States are different. One of them may be right for you!

Students at St. John's College take classes at two campuses on opposite sides of the country! The college has a campus in Annapolis, Maryland, in the east and in Santa Fe, New Mexico, in the west. All the students must study the works of the world's greatest writers and thinkers such as Homer, Plato, and Einstein. They must also study ancient Greek, modern French, and English poetry. Classes are very small, and students take few tests. Instead, they have class discussions and write papers.

Cornell College in Iowa is a different kind of college, too. Traditional colleges have two semesters each year, but Cornell College has eight semesters! Each semester is only three and a half weeks, and students take only one class each semester. The teachers there believe students can learn better when they only concentrate on one class at a time.

The College of the Ozarks in Missouri is another nontraditional college. The directors of this college understand that many students cannot pay tuition. The College of the Ozarks charges no tuition. Instead, it has a work program and helps students find jobs. All students work for the school for 15 hours per week. In addition, students must work full-time (40 hours per week) between semesters. As a result, students can pay for their education through the work program.

There are many other nontraditional colleges in the United States and all over the world. Which one is the right college for you?

The College of the Ozarks campus in Missouri

QUESTIONS FOR ANOTHER LOOK

1. What are two ways that St. John's College is nontraditional?

   ____

2. How are the semesters at Cornell College different from semesters at a traditional college?

   ____

3. How can students go to the College of the Ozarks if they do not have enough money?

   ____

Topics for Discussion and Writing

1. Do you want to go to college? Why or why not? What are your reasons for this?
2. Do you think video applications are a good way for colleges to get new students? Why or why not?
3. Imagine you can go to St. John's College, Cornell College, or the College of the Ozarks. Which one do you prefer? Why?
4. Write in your journal. Describe your plans for the future. What will you do? Where will you go?

Critical Thinking

1. Work with one or two classmates. Create a nontraditional college. In what ways will your college be nontraditional? Why will students want to study there?
2. Use your cell phone to make a short video of yourself. Answer these questions: Who are you? Are you different from other students? Why? Then share your video with your classmates.
3. Discuss this question with a partner: Is it important for everyone to go to college? Why or why not?

Crossword Puzzle

Review the words in the box below. Then read the clues on the next page. Write the words in the correct spaces in the puzzle.

advantage	essay	SAT	traditional
application	freshman	simpler	transcript
attract	official	stressful	video
complicated	recommendation	TOEFL	

1 2 3 4 5 6 7 8 9 10 11 12 13 14

Crossword Puzzle Clues

ACROSS CLUES

2. When you want to go to college, you need to fill out an ________ form.
4. A ________ semester is 15 weeks long.
6. Sometimes the forms to go to a college are very ________, and not simple at all.
8. Many students think that applying to college is very ________ because it is so long and hard to do.
11. You can ask a teacher or an employer to write a letter of ________ for you.
13. The ________ is a test that American students take when they apply to college.
14. An ________ is something that is helpful to you.

DOWN CLUES

1. When you apply to some colleges, you need to write an ________.
3. When you apply to most colleges, you need to send an ________ record of your courses and grades.
4. The ________ is a test that shows a student's ability to understand and use English in college.
5. A ________ is a record of your courses and grades that a school or college sends to another school or college.
7. A student is called a ________ during his or her first year at college.
9. For some students, it is much ________ to make a two-minute film than it is to fill out a long form.
10. Every college wants to ________ good students to its school.
12. Goucher College only requires a two-minute ________ when you apply there.

UNIT 2 Family Life

At a Chinese New Year dinner celebration, a family throws food into the air and asks for good luck for the year.

1. How many people are in your family? Do you have a big family or a small family?
2. Does your family have a healthy diet? Why or why not? Explain.

CHAPTER 3 How alike are identical twins?

Prereading

1. Look at the photo. Describe the two people.

2. Read the title of this chapter. What will the reading tell you about?

3. Which sentences describe identical twins? Check (√) all that apply.

_____ a. They are always both boys or both girls.
_____ b. Identical twins can be a boy and a girl.
_____ c. Identical twins always have the same color hair.
_____ d. One identical twin can have dark hair and the other can have light hair.
_____ e. Identical twins always have the same color eyes.
_____ f. One identical twin may have blue eyes and the other may have brown eyes.
_____ g. As adults, identical twins will be the same height.
_____ h. As adults, one identical twin may be taller than the other.

Reading

CD 1
TR 6

Read the following passage carefully. Then complete the exercises that follow.

How alike are identical twins?

Most twins who grow up together are very close. John and Buell Fuller are 79-year-old identical twins. They have always lived together, and still do. They wear identical clothes and work together, too. They think it is funny that people can't tell them apart. In fact, they like to confuse people. Sometimes John tells people he is Buell, and sometimes Buell tells people he is John.

Identical twins like the Fullers are very unusual in the United States. Out of every 1,000 births, there are only four pairs of identical twins, although there are many more pairs of fraternal twins.[1] Naturally, most people are very curious about identical twins. Scientists want to know about identical twins, too. Do they feel the same pain? Do they think the same thoughts? Do they share these thoughts?

Scientists understand how identical twins are born. Now, though, they are trying to explain how being half of a biological pair influences a twin's identity. They want to know why many identical twins make similar choices even when they don't live near each other. For example, Jim Springer and Jim Lewis are identical twins. They were separated when they were only four months old.

The two Jims grew up in different families and did not meet for 39 years. When they finally met, they discovered some surprising similarities between them. Both men were married twice. Their first wives were named Linda, and their second wives were both named Betty! Both twins named their first sons James Allan, drove blue Chevrolets, and had dogs named Toy. Are all these facts coincidences, or are they biological?

Scientists want to know what influences our personality. They study pairs of identical twins who grew up in different surroundings, like Jim Springer and Jim Lewis. These twins help scientists understand the connection between environment and biology. Researchers at the University of Minnesota studied 350 sets of identical twins who did not grow up together. They discovered many similarities in their personalities. Scientists believe that personality characteristics, such as friendliness, shyness, and fearfulness, are not a result of environment. Instead, people probably inherit these characteristics.

Some pairs of identical twins say that they have ESP[2] experiences. For instance, some twins say that they can feel when their twin is in pain or in trouble. Twins also

---

[1]Identical twins are two children born at the same time, have the same mother, and are exactly the same. Fraternal twins are also two children born at the same time and have the same mother, but they may look different and may not be the same sex.

[2]ESP: Extrasensory perception. ESP is the ability to feel something that people cannot feel with the five senses.

seem to be closer and more open to each other's thoughts and feelings than other brothers and sisters. For example, Donald and Louis Keith are close in this way. The Keiths are identical twins. Donald says that by concentrating very hard, he can make Louis telephone him.

Scientists continue to study identical twins because they are uncertain about them and have many questions. For example, they are still unsure about the connection between environment and personality. They want to know: Can twins really communicate without speaking? Can one twin really feel another twin's pain? Perhaps with more research, scientists will find the answers.

Identical twins in Umri Village near Allahabad

Fact Finding

Read the passage again. Then read the following statements. Check (√) whether each statement is True or False. If a statement is false, rewrite it so that it is true. Then go back to the passage and find the line that supports your answer.

1. _____ True _____ False Scientists want to know about identical twins.

____

2. _____ True _____ False Jim Springer and Jim Lewis have always lived together.

____

3. _____ True _____ False Scientists understand twins better when they study twins who grew up together.

____

4. _____ True _____ False John and Buell Fuller were separated at birth and did not grow up together.

____

5. _____ True _____ False Some identical twins have ESP experiences about each other.

____

6. _____ True _____ False Scientists believe that people are born with friendly, shy, or fearful personalities.

____

Reading Analysis

Read each question carefully. Circle the letter or the number of the correct answer, or write your answer in the space provided.

1. Most twins who grew up together are very **close**. John and Buell Fuller are 79-year-old identical twins. They have always lived together, and **still do**. They wear identical clothes and work together, too. They think it is funny that people **can't tell them apart**.

a. In this paragraph, **close** means that they

1. look the same.
2. live in the same house.
3. are very good friends.

b. What do John and Buell Fuller **still do**?
   1. Confuse people
   2. Live together
   3. Wear the same clothes

c. People **can't tell them apart**.
   This means that
   1. they look exactly the same.
   2. people can't talk to them alone.
   3. they never live apart.

2. **Out of every 1,000 births, there are only four pairs of identical twins**, although there are many more pairs of **fraternal** twins.

a. The first part of this sentence means that
   1. if 1,000 women have babies, four women will have identical twins.
   2. only four pairs of identical twins are born in the United States every year.

b. Look at page 35. **Fraternal** twins are different from identical twins because
   1. fraternal twins may not look exactly the same or be the same sex.
   2. fraternal twins cannot be both boys or both girls.
   3. fraternal twins never have the same mother.

c. How do you know this information about fraternal twins?
   1. This information is in my dictionary.
   2. My classmate told me this information.
   3. This information is in a footnote.

3. **Naturally**, most people **are very curious** about identical twins. Scientists want to know about twins, too. Do twins feel the same pain? Do they think the same thoughts? Do they share these thoughts?

a. **Naturally** means
   1. however.
   2. of course.
   3. additionally.

b. In these sentences, which word or phrase is a synonym for **are very curious**?
   1. Feel
   2. Want to know
   3. Think

4. Scientists understand how twins are born. Now, though, they are trying to explain how **being half of a biological pair** influences a twin's **identity**.

a. **Being half of a biological pair** means being
   1. a scientist.
   2. a twin.
   3. alone.

b. Your **identity** is
   1. who you are.
   2. being a twin.
   3. where you live.

5. Jim Springer and Jim Lewis are famous identical twins. They were separated when they were only four months old. The **two Jims** grew up in different families and did not meet for 39 years. **Both** men were married twice. Their first wives were named Linda, and their second wives were **both** named Betty!

a. Who are the **two Jims**?

____

b. How many is **both**?
   1. Two
   2. Four
   3. Six

6. Both twins named their first sons James Allan, drove blue Chevrolets, and had dogs named Toy. Are all these facts simply **coincidences**, or are they biological?

a. A **coincidence** is something that happens
   1. by plan or arrangement.
   2. by accident or chance.

b. Read the following sentences. Decide which situation is a coincidence and circle the number of the correct answer.
   1. Dean telephoned Jenny and invited her to have lunch with him. They decided to meet at one o'clock in front of The Palace Restaurant. Jenny arrived at one o'clock, and Dean arrived at 1:05. They said hi to each other and went into the restaurant.
   2. Dean and Jenny sat at a table in the restaurant. Jenny saw her sister, Christine, at the next table! Jenny and Christine greeted each other, and they all had lunch together at the same table.

7. Scientists want to know what influences our personality. They study **pairs** of identical twins who grew up in different **surroundings**, like Jim Springer and Jim Lewis. These twins help scientists understand the connection between environment and biology. Researchers at the University of Minnesota studied 350 sets of identical twins who did not grow up together.

a. In this paragraph, which word is a synonym for **pairs**?

____

b. In this paragraph, which word is a synonym for **surroundings**?

____

c. **Surroundings** means
   1. the house you live in.
   2. the place you live in.
   3. the people you live with.
   4. All of the above

8. Scientists believe that personality characteristics, such as friendliness, shyness, and fearfulness, are not a result of environment. Instead, people probably **inherit** these characteristics.

a. What are some examples of personality characteristics?

____

b. How do you know?

____

c. Something **inherited**

1. comes from your parents.
2. comes from the environment.
3. comes from learning.

9. Some pairs of identical twins say that they have **ESP** experiences.

a. Look at page 35. What is **ESP**?

____

b. How do you know?

____

10. For example, Donald and Louis Keith are very close in this way. **The Keiths** are identical twins. Donald says that by **concentrating** very hard, he can make Louis telephone him.

a. Who are **the Keiths**?

____

b. What does Donald mean when he says this?

1. When Donald tells Louis to call him, Louis calls him.
2. When Donald thinks about Louis, Louis calls him.

c. When you **concentrate** on something, you

1. think very hard about it.
2. tell someone about it.
3. call someone to talk about it.

11. Scientists continue to study identical twins because they are **uncertain** about them and have many questions. For example: They are unsure about the connection between environment and personality.

In this paragraph, what word means the same as **uncertain**?

____

12. What is the main idea of this passage?

a. John and Buell Fuller, typical identical twins, grew up together.
b. Identical twins are very unusual in the United States.
c. Doctors believe that identical twins are very similar in both their looks and their personalities.

Vocabulary Skills

PART 1

Recognizing Word Forms

In English, some adjectives become nouns by adding the suffix *-ness,* for example, *loud (adj.), loudness (n.).* Some words change spelling, for example, *happy (adj.), happiness (n.).*

Complete each sentence with the correct word form on the left. The nouns are all singular.

close *(adj.)*	**1.** John and Buell Fuller are very ____________ and tell each other everything.
closeness *(n.)*	Their ____________ will continue for many years.
sure *(adj.)*	**2.** Researchers are not ____________ that people inherit personality traits.
sureness *(n.)*	Identical twins help them understand the ____________ of this theory.
open *(adj.)*	**3.** Jim Lewis and Jim Springer both have a special ____________ that many
openness *(n.)*	people like. They make friends easily with their warm, ____________
	personalities.
friendly *(adj.)*	**4.** The Fullers are very ____________. Because of their ____________, people
friendliness *(n.)*	are very comfortable with them.
shy *(adj.)*	**5.** Personality characteristics, such as ____________, may be inherited. A person
shyness *(n.)*	can be ____________ because his mother or father is the same way.

PART 2

Understanding Antonyms

Antonyms are words that have opposite meanings. For example, *night* and *day* are antonyms.

Match each word with its antonym. Write the letter of the correct answer and the word in the space provided.

d. neither	1. both	a. apart
______	2. coincidence	b. common
______	3. curious	c. different
______	4. separate	~~d. neither~~
______	5. similar	e. plan
______	6. together	f. sure
______	7. uncertain	g. together
______	8. unusual	h. uninterested

Vocabulary in Context

Read the following sentences. Complete each sentence with the correct word from the box. Use each word only once.

both *(adj.)*	coincidence *(n.)*	curious *(adj.)*	identical *(adj.)*
close *(adj.)*	concentrate *(v.)*	environment *(n.)*	uncertain *(adj.)*

1. Yesterday I saw our teacher on the bus. It was a ______________. She was going to the movies, and I was going to the library.

2. I like to study in my room or at the library because ______________ places are very quiet.

3. I need to ______________ very hard when I do my homework, so I never listen to music when I study.

4. Leigh and her sister are very ______________. They share everything and go everywhere together.

5. I am ______________________ about the weather today. It may rain, so I will bring my umbrella to school.

6. Our reading books are ______________________. They are exactly the same.

7. John loves going to the mountains. It is a very quiet, healthy ______________________.

8. I was very ______________________ about our new classmate, so I asked her some questions. She was very happy to tell me about herself.

Reading Skill

Understanding a Bar Graph

Bar graphs often contain important information. It's important to understand bar graphs. Bar graphs compare numbers or amount and give you information about the reading.

Look at the bar graphs below and answer the questions.

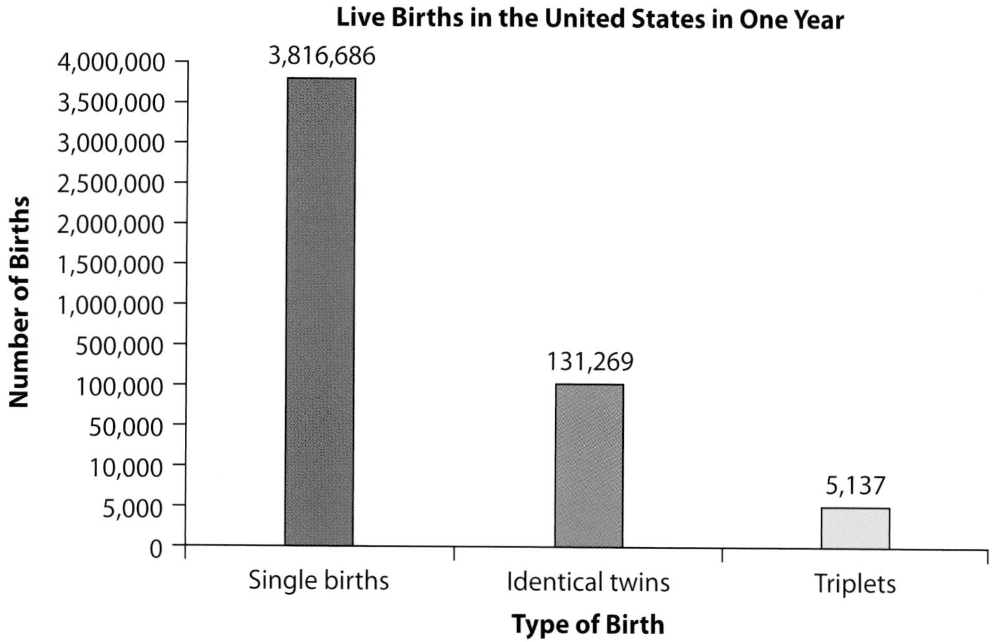

Source: http://www.nomotc.org/index.php?option=com_content&task=view&id=66&Itemid=55

1. Which of the following sentences are true? Put a check (√) next to them.

   a. ______ There are more single births than identical twins.
   b. ______ There are more identical twins than single births.
   c. ______ There are more triplets than identical twins.
   d. ______ There are more triplets than single births.
   e. ______ There are more identical twins than triplets.

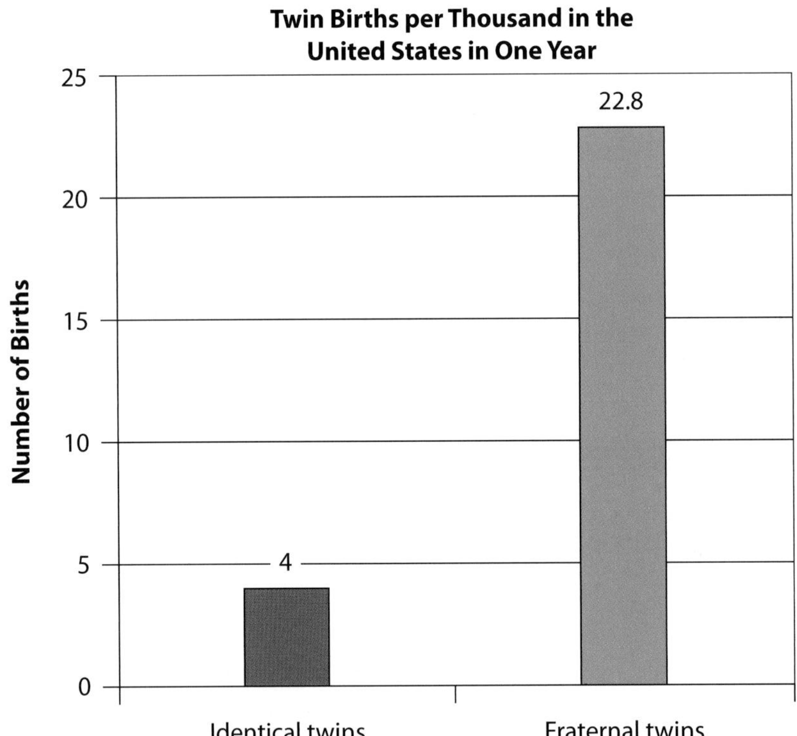

Source: http://www.nomotc.org/index.php?option=com_content&task=view&id=67&Itemid=55

2. What information does this bar graph show?

   a. The number of all births in the United States in one year
   b. The number of all twin births in one year
   c. The number of twin births for every one thousand births

Another Look

CD 1 TR 7

Read a father's diary about the birth of his triplets and their life experiences. Then answer the questions that follow.

Diary of a Father of Triplets

Birth to Six Months

When the doctor told us that we were pregnant with triplets, we were surprised and wondered what the future would be like. We quickly found out after we brought our three babies home.

The first six months of parenthood is a difficult learning experience. We wrote everything down, especially feeding times and how much food the babies ate. We even had to chart diaper changes (960 the first month!). We marked all the toys, bottles, and clothes with a different color for each child so they could sense what was theirs.

Six Months to Four Years

It was hardest for us to get used to all the equipment. We had three of everything: car seats, portable cribs, high chairs, diaper bags, and changes of clothes, not to mention toys!

At this time of life, every minute is a new discovery. Even though you try very hard, you will never be able to carefully watch all three of them at once! Every two-year-old must touch and taste everything, but everything must also be shared by the triplets. We soon learned that they each wanted whatever his or her siblings had at that moment.

When they began to speak, my wife noticed that they had their own names for each other. When we began to make note of the particular sounds that they said to each other, we realized that they had their own language. The age that we have the happiest memories of is two.

School Age

When it was time to send the children to school, they went to three different classes. Kindergarten and first grade were easier for the kids than they were for us. They each had plenty of arts and crafts homework. Since they had three different assignments, homework lasted a long time. Second grade seems to be less of a problem at homework time because they are able to do more work without our help.

The triplets don't always get along. Sometimes they fight just like other brothers and sisters. However, there is still a bond between them that my wife and I hope never disappears.

A family with triplets

QUESTIONS FOR ANOTHER LOOK

Read the following list of life experiences. Write the number of each under the correct age category in the chart below.

1. Homework lasted a long time because they had different assignments.
2. The triplets had their own language.
3. The parents wrote down feeding times and how much food each baby ate.
4. It was hard for the parents to get used to all the equipment.
5. The parents wrote down diaper changes.
6. Homework time became easier in second grade because the triplets needed less help.
7. The triplets touched and tasted everything.
8. The triplets had their own names for each other.
9. The parents marked all toys, clothes, and bottles with a different color.
10. Each triplet wanted whatever his or her siblings had.
11. The triplets each went to different kindergarten classes.

Birth to Six Months	Six Months to Four Years	School Age

Topics for Discussion and Writing

1. Do you know any twins or triplets? Write about them. Tell who they are. Describe how they are alike and how they are different.
2. Explain and give reasons why you think being a twin may be both a positive and a negative experience.
3. Write in your journal. Imagine that you have a twin brother or sister. What do you like best about having a twin? What do you like least about having a twin?

Identical twins in matching outfits

Critical Thinking

1. Work with a partner. Imagine you are going to interview a set of identical twins. These twins *did not* grow up together. In fact, they did not meet until they were 30 years old. Write a list of questions to ask the twins. You want to find out how they are similar and different. Compare your list of questions with those of your classmates.

2. Work with a partner. Imagine you are going to interview a set of identical twins. These twins *did* grow up together. Write a list of questions to ask the twins. You want to find out how they are similar and different. Compare your list of questions with those of your classmates.

3. If you can find a set of twins or triplets, interview them. Use the questions from activities 1 and 2 above. Report back to the class.

4. Scientists want to study identical twins who did not grow up together. They want to understand the connection between environment and biology. Why are these identical twins so helpful to scientists? Discuss this question with a partner. Then compare your answers with those of your classmates.

5. Scientists believe that friendliness, shyness, and fearfulness are inherited. What personality characteristics do you think are the result of environment? Discuss your answers with your classmates.

Crossword Puzzle

Review the words in the box below. Then read the clues on the next page. Write the words in the correct spaces in the puzzle.

apart	concentrate	identical	pair
biological	curious	identity	still
both	ESP	inherited	surroundings
close	fraternal	naturally	uncertain
coincidence			

Crossword Puzzle Clues

ACROSS CLUES

1. Twins are always a _________. There are always two of them.
5. I saw identical twin girls yesterday. _________ girls had on white shirts, blue skirts, and blue shoes.
7. _________ means not sure.
11. Our _________ are everything around us.
12. _________ means exactly the same.
13. Kathy and Laura are very good friends. They are very _________.
14. I am learning a lot about twins, but I am _________ interested in learning more.
15. Your _________ is your character. It is who you are.
16. _________ is the ability to feel something that other people feel but without using your five senses.

DOWN CLUES

2. Your hair color and your eye color are _________ from your parents.
3. Some twins do not like to be _________. They like being together all the time.
4. A _________ is something that happens accidentally, without planning.
5. Michael is my _________ brother. We have the same mother and father.
6. When I think very hard about something, I _________ on it.
8. _________ means surely, of course.
9. Luis and Maria are _________ twins. They were born on the same day and have the same mother, but one is a boy and the other is a girl.
10. I am very _________ about twins. Do they think alike?

CHAPTER 4 A Healthy Diet for You and Your Family

Prereading

Discuss these questions with a partner.

1. Look at the photos. Describe the two meals. Which meal do you think is healthier? Why?
2. What kinds of food do you think are healthy? What kinds of food are not? Fill in the chart below.

Healthy	Not Healthy

3. Why is it important to have a healthy diet?

4. Read the title of this chapter. People in different cultures and countries eat different kinds of food. Do people in your culture have a healthy diet? Why or why not? What changes can your family make to have a healthy diet?

Reading

Read the following passage carefully. Then complete the exercises that follow.

A Healthy Diet for You and Your Family

Everyone knows that we must eat in order to live. However, sometimes people are confused about what types of food are healthy and what kinds of food can be harmful to our health. About 20 years ago, the USDA[1] prepared a food guide to help people learn about which types of food are the healthiest for themselves and their families. The food guide described six basic food groups: meat (beef, fish, chicken, and beans, too), dairy (milk, yogurt, cheese, etc.), grains (bread, cereal, rice, etc.), fruit, and vegetables. The last group was fats, oils, and sweets. The USDA also suggested how much of each food group is healthy to eat daily. This guide was helpful, but it was also confusing. Recently, the U.S. government replaced this guide with a newer, easier one. It is called "My Plate."[2]

As a result of years of research, we now know that too much animal fat is bad for our health. For example, many Americans eat a lot of meat and only a small amount of grains, fruit, and vegetables. Because of their diet, they have a high rate of cancer and heart disease. In Japan, in contrast, people eat large amounts of grains and very little meat. The Japanese also have a very low rate of cancer and heart disease. In fact, the Japanese live longer than almost anyone else in the world. Unfortunately, when Japanese people move to the United States, their rate of heart disease and cancer increases as their diet changes. Moreover, as hamburgers, ice cream, and other foods high in fat are becoming popular in Japan, the rate of heart disease and cancer is increasing there as well. People are also eating more meat and dairy products in other countries, such as Cuba, Mauritius, and Hungary. Not surprisingly, the disease rate

[1]**USDA:** The United States Department of Agriculture. The USDA's responsibility is to control the quality of food in the United States.

[2]Refer to the chart on page 65 for information on My Plate.

in these countries is increasing along with the change in diet. Consequently, doctors everywhere advise people to eat more grains, fruit, and vegetables, and eat less meat and fewer dairy products.

Of course a healthy diet is important for all family members—children as well as adults. Most of us learn good eating habits from our parents. When parents have poor eating habits, their children usually do, too. After all, most families eat meals together, and children eat the same way their parents do. When parents eat healthy food, their children will learn to enjoy it, and they will develop good eating habits. Doctors advise parents to give their children healthier snacks such as fruit, vegetables, and juice.

Everyone wants to live a long, healthy life. We know that the food we eat affects us in different ways. For instance, doctors believe that fruit and vegetables can actually prevent many diseases. On the other hand, animal fat can cause some diseases. We can improve our diet now and enjoy many years of healthy living.

A family enjoys a healthy meal together.

Fact Finding

Read the passage again. Then read the following statements. Check (√) whether each statment is True or False. If a statement is false, rewrite it so that it is true. Then go back to the passage and find the line that supports your answer.

1. _____ True _____ False There were six basic food groups in the USDA food guide.

   ____

2. _____ True _____ False Most Americans eat a lot of meat.

   ____

3. _____ True _____ False Most Japanese eat very few grains.

   ____

4. _____ True _____ False There is a high rate of cancer and heart disease in Japan.

   ____

5. _____ True _____ False Doctors think it is a good idea for people to eat less meat.

   ____

6. _____ True _____ False It is not important for children to have a healthy diet.

   ____

7. _____ True _____ False Children usually eat differently than their parents.

   ____

8. _____ True _____ False Doctors believe that fruit and vegetables cause different diseases.

   ____

Reading Analysis

Read each question carefully. Circle the letter or the number of the correct answer or write your answer in the space provided.

1. Everyone knows that we must eat **in order to** live.

a. What information follows **in order to**?

1. The reason
2. The decision
3. The cause

b. Complete the following sentence with the appropriate choice.
Cindy went to the supermarket in order to

1. walk to the store.
2. learn how to cook.
3. buy some food.

2. Sometimes people are **confused** about what types of food are healthy and what **kinds** of food can be **harmful** to our health.

a. In this sentence, which word is a synonym for **kinds**?

____

b. **Confused** means

1. uncertain.
2. clear.
3. unhappy.

c. **Harmful** means

1. bad.
2. good.
3. easy.

3. About 20 years ago, the **USDA** prepared a food guide to help families learn about which types of food are the healthiest to eat. The food guide described six **basic food groups**: meat (beef, fish, chicken, and beans, too), dairy (milk, yogurt, cheese, etc.), grains (bread, cereal, rice, etc.), fruit, and vegetables. The last group was fats, oils, and sweets. The USDA also suggested how much of each food group is healthy to eat **daily**.

a. Refer to page 53. What is the **USDA**?

____

b. What are the **basic food groups**? Give examples of each group.

1. ______________________________________
2. ______________________________________

3. ______________________________

4. ______________________________

5. ______________________________

6. ______________________________

c. **Daily** means
   1. every day.
   2. a lot of.
   3. a little of.

4. Many Americans eat a lot of meat and only a small amount of grains, fruit, and vegetables. In Japan, **in contrast**, people eat large amounts of grains and very little meat. The Japanese also have a very low rate of cancer and heart disease. **In fact**, the Japanese live longer than **anyone else** in the world.

a. What information follows **in contrast**?
   1. A similar idea
   2. An opposite idea
   3. The same idea

b. What information follows **in fact**?
   1. More information about the same idea
   2. Contrasting information about the same idea
   3. Surprising information about the same idea

c. **Anyone else** means
   1. all other people.
   2. some other people.
   3. most other people.

5. **Unfortunately**, when Japanese people move to the United States, their rate of heart disease and cancer increases **as** their diet changes. **Moreover**, as hamburgers, ice cream, and other foods high in fat are becoming popular in Japan, the rate of heart disease and cancer is increasing **there**, as well.

a. What follows **unfortunately**?
   1. Something good
   2. Something bad
   3. Something false

b. **As** means
   1. when.
   2. so.
   3. and.

c. **Moreover** means
   1. however.
   2. also.
   3. then.

d. What are some examples of foods high in fat?

____

e. Where does **there** refer to?
   1. In the United States
   2. In Cuba
   3. In Japan

6. People are also eating more meat and dairy products in other countries, **such as** Cuba, Mauritius, and Hungary. **Not surprisingly**, the disease rate in these countries is increasing along with the change in diet. **Consequently**, doctors everywhere advise people to eat more grains, fruit, and vegetables, and eat less meat and fewer dairy products.

a. **Such as** means
   1. for example.
   2. instead of.
   3. except in.

b. What information follows **not surprisingly**?
   1. Information that is hard to believe
   2. Information that is not true
   3. Information that is easy to believe

c. **Consequently** means
   1. in addition.
   2. as a result.
   3. in fact.

7. A healthy diet is important for children **as well as** adults.

a. This sentence means that a healthy diet
   1. is more important for children than it is for adults.
   2. is more important for adults than it is for children.
   3. is equally important for both adults and children.

b. **As well as** means
   1. and also.
   2. but not.
   3. instead of.

8. When parents have poor eating habits, their children usually do, too.
After all, most families eat meals together, and children eat the same way their parents do.

a. The first sentence means that
   1. the children usually have better eating habits.
   2. the children also have poor eating habits.

b. Read the second sentence again. Then read the following sentence and circle the number of the choice that best completes it.
   John speaks Spanish fluently. **After all**,
   1. he lived in Venezuela for 15 years.
   2. he reads many books about South America.

9. For instance, most doctors agree that fruit and vegetables can actually **prevent** many diseases. **On the other hand**, animal fat can **cause** some diseases.

a. What is the connection between **prevent** and **cause**?
   1. They have similar meanings.
   2. They have opposite meanings.

b. **Prevent** means
   1. to keep from happening.
   2. to make happen.

c. What information follows **on the other hand**?
   1. A similar idea
   2. An example of the idea
   3. An opposite idea

d. Read the following sentences. Then circle the number of the choice that best completes the second sentence.
   I may visit many different places on my vacation. On the other hand,
   1. I may go to museums, zoos, parks, and beaches.
   2. I may stay at home and relax.

10. What is the main idea of this passage?

a. The kind of diet we have can cause or prevent diseases.
b. Doctors advise people to eat more fruit, vegetables, and grains.
c. Eating meat causes cancer and heart disease.

Vocabulary Skills

PART 1

Recognizing Word Forms

In English, some verbs become nouns by adding the suffix *-ment*, for example, *announce (v.), announcement (n.)*.

Complete each sentence with the correct word form on the left. Write all the verbs in the simple present. The nouns are all singular.

improve *(v.)*	**1.** We may live longer when we ____________ our diets. A small ____________
improvement *(n.)*	in the way we eat can be very important.

agree *(v.)* **2.** Doctors are in ____________ that some kinds of fruit and vegetables can
agreement *(n.)* prevent disease. They also ____________ that some kinds of food can cause disease.

encourage *(v.)* **3.** Parents ____________ their children to have healthy diets. The parents'
encouragement *(n.)* ____________ is very important to the children.

develop *(v.)* **4.** The ____________ of good eating habits can start at a very young age.
development *(n.)* Children ____________ these habits when their parents eat healthy food.

enjoy *(v.)* **5.** Children usually ____________ the same food that their parents do. They can
enjoyment *(n.)* be healthy because of their ____________ of healthy food.

PART 2

Understanding Synonyms

Synonyms are words with similar meanings. For example, *sad* and *unhappy* are synonyms.

Match each word or phrase with its synonym. Write the letter of the correct answer and the word or phrase in the space provided.

e. also	1. as well as	a. unluckily
____________	2. such as	b. actually
____________	3. consequently	c. furthermore
____________	4. in contrast	d. so that
____________	5. moreover	~~e. also~~
____________	6. unfortunately	f. for example
____________	7. in order to	g. on the other hand
____________	8. in fact	h. as a result

Vocabulary in Context

Read the following sentences. Complete each sentence with the correct word or phrase from the box. Use each word or phrase only once.

confuse *(v.)*	in order to	suggest *(v.)*
in contrast	not surprisingly *(adv.)*	unfortunately *(adv.)*
in fact	prevent *(v.)*	

1. Leon eats fresh fruit and vegetables daily. His brother, Sam, eats cake and cookies every day. ____________________, Leon is healthier than Sam.
2. Viola wanted to go swimming at the beach yesterday. ____________________, it rained all day, so she stayed home.
3. Mark and his brother, Tom, look very different. Mark is short and has light hair. ____________________, Tom is tall and has dark hair.
4. When Harry and Bill do dangerous work, they ____________________ injury by being especially careful.
5. Jane loves to read. ____________________, she reads about 100 books a year.
6. If you want to get up at 4:00 a.m. to go fishing, I ____________________ that you go to bed before 8:00 p.m.
7. ____________________ lose weight, you need to exercise more and eat less.
8. Linda's directions always ____________________ me. When she gives me directions, I usually get lost.

Reading Skill

Creating a Flowchart

Flowcharts show certain kinds of information—such as cause and effect—and how people come to conclusions. Creating a flowchart can help you organize and understand important information from a reading passage.

Read the passage on pages 53 and 54 again. Then complete the flowchart below.

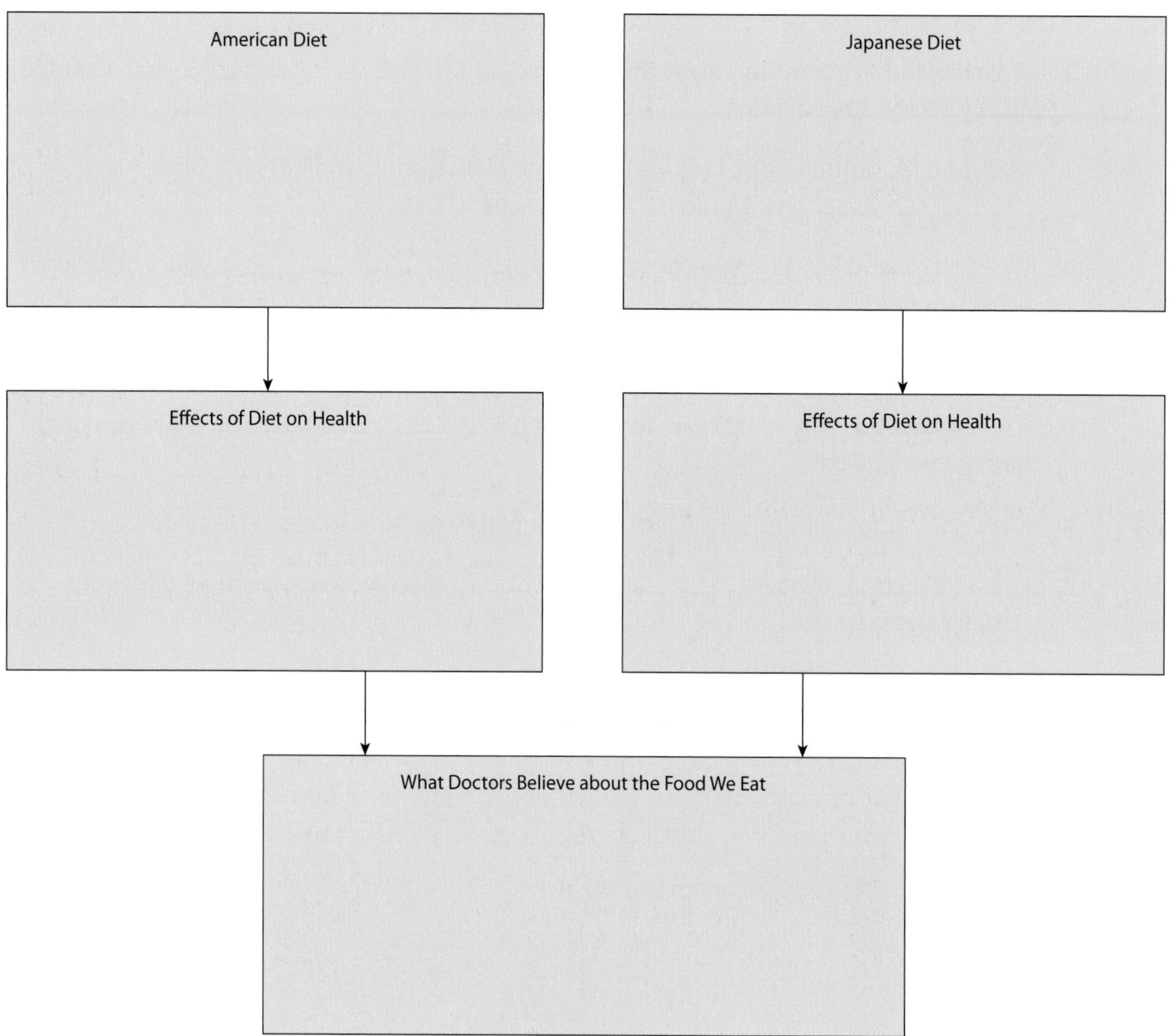

Another Look

CD 1 TR 9

Read the following passage about reasons why people eat when they're not hungry. Then answer the questions that follow.

Why do I eat when I'm not hungry?

The next time you want to eat something, ask yourself this question: "Am I really hungry?" If you answer no, then ask yourself why you want to eat when your body is not really hungry. The following reasons may help you understand why you do so.

- I'M BORED. Sometimes we are bored and don't have anything better to do. The next time you feel this way and you start walking toward the kitchen, stop yourself. Go to another part of the house, or go outside for a walk.
- IT TASTES GOOD. Sometimes it does, but sometimes we eat anything we can find in the kitchen, even if it really isn't that great tasting. When I'm dieting, I like to eat food that I *really* enjoy. Eat less of it and enjoy it.
- I HAVE A LOT OF STRESS. This is often a common reason for eating. I often eat because of stress, not because I am hungry. When you feel stressed, don't eat. Read a book or exercise instead.
- TV MAKES ME WANT TO EAT. I rarely watched TV when I was thin. Then I started to watch TV almost every evening, and I gained 45 pounds. Evening TV programs have many food commercials that make you want to run to the kitchen for a snack. My best advice is to stop watching evening television.
- BECAUSE I'M REALLY THIRSTY. Sometimes people eat because they are thirsty. Instead of having something to drink, people eat something that is often fattening. So the next time you feel hungry, drink some water first.

If your stomach is making noise, it is time to eat. If you want food between meals when your stomach is not making noise, don't eat. Remember, you should give your body some kind of nutrition three times a day. If you do have to eat between meals, eat a piece of fruit or some vegetables. Try to think about what and why you are eating the next time you want a snack. Ask yourself, "Why am I eating?"

QUESTIONS FOR ANOTHER LOOK

1. What is the main idea of the passage?
   a. There are many reasons why people eat when they are hungry.
   b. There are many reasons why people eat when they are not hungry.
   c. Watching television makes people eat when they are not hungry.

2. What are some reasons why people eat when they are not hungry?

   ____

   ____

   ____

   ____

   ____

3. Instead of eating when you are not hungry, what are some other things you can do?

   ____

   ____

   ____

   ____

Topics for Discussion and Writing

1. Is there a high rate of heart disease or cancer in your country? What do you think are some reasons for this?

2. The reading passage discusses a healthy diet as a way to prevent disease. Work with a classmate. Make a list of other ways to prevent disease. Compare your list with those of your classmates.

3. Do you have children? What kinds of food do you give them? Why? Do they enjoy them? If you don't have children, imagine that you do. What kinds of food would you give them? Why?

4. Write in your journal. Describe the ways you help yourself live a healthy life.

Critical Thinking

1. The USDA designed "My Plate" to help people choose healthy meals for themselves and their families. Look at the graphic below.

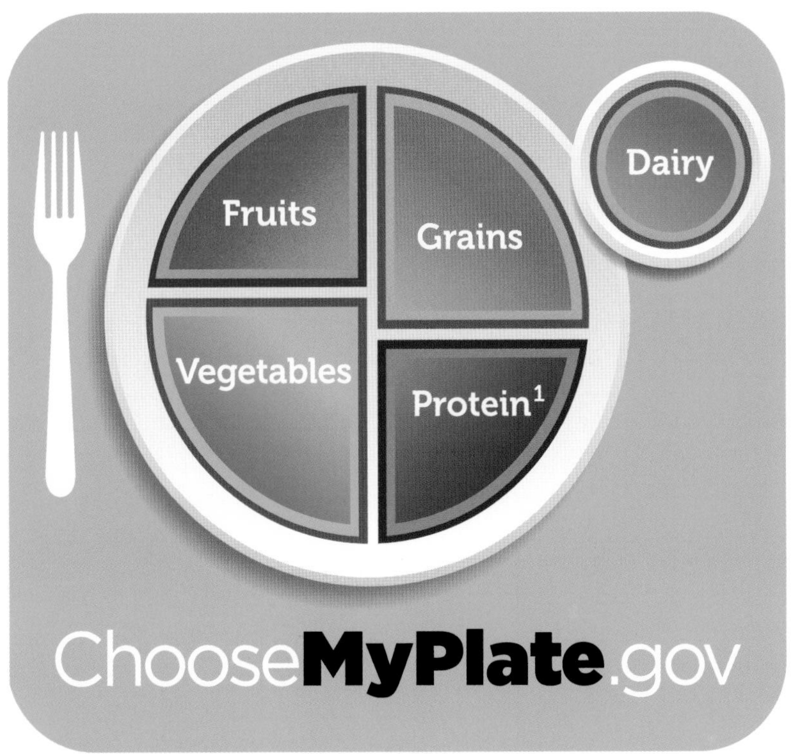

Source: http://www.choosemyplate.gov/
[1]Protein is a substance in most food. We need some protein for a healthy diet.

a. Below is a list of different kinds of high-protein food and low-protein food. Check (√) the kinds of food that are high in protein.

1. ______ potatoes
2. ______ beef
3. ______ milk
4. ______ fruit
5. ______ eggs
6. ______ carrots
7. ______ beans
8. ______ corn
9. ______ chicken
10. ______ nuts

b. Use "My Plate" to plan a one-day healthy diet. Write your diet in the chart below.

A One-Day Healthy Diet		
Breakfast	(Snack)	Lunch
(Snack)	Dinner	(Snack)

c. Compare your one-day healthy diet with those of your classmates. In what ways are they similar? In what ways are they different?

2. Work with a partner. Larry is a college student. The following menu shows what he usually eats for breakfast, lunch, and dinner. What changes can you make to Larry's diet in order to make it healthier for him?

Breakfast:	***Lunch:***
two eggs two slices of white bread with butter one cup of coffee with cream and sugar	one large chocolate ice-cream cone
Dinner:	***Late-night snack:***
one cheeseburger on a roll one large order of French fries an order of broccoli lettuce and tomatoes	a bag of potato chips an apple

3. Alone or with another student from your country, prepare a menu for a typical breakfast, lunch, and dinner for a family in your country. Then talk to a classmate from another country, and show him or her your menu. Explain why you think your diet is healthy. Then ask the other student to explain why he or she thinks his or her diet is healthy. Discuss which diet you both think is healthier.

4. Go to a fast-food restaurant with a friend. Order a healthy meal. Report back to the class. Describe the meal you ate, and explain why it was nutritious.

5. Discuss this question with a partner: Why did the USDA make "My Plate" for Americans?

6. Why do Japanese people change their diet when they move to the United States? Do you think many people change their diet when they move to a new county?

Crossword Puzzle

Review the words in the box below. Then read the clues on the next page. Write the words in the correct spaces in the puzzle.

as	contrast	harmful	surprisingly
basic	daily	kind	unfortunately
cause	else	moreover	USDA
confused	fact	order	
consequently	hand	prevent	

Crossword Puzzle Clues

ACROSS CLUES

3. Let's make a list of the kinds of food that may be ________ to our health and make sure we do not eat them.

5. The Japanese often live a long time. In ________, they live longer than people in any other country.

7. That child eats too much cake and candy. Not ________, he is overweight.

9. We need food and air in ________ to live.

12. Yolanda drinks more coffee than anyone ________ I know.

13. The ________ controls the quality of food in the United States.

14. What ________ of fruit do you like to eat?

15. People can become healthier or less healthy ________ their diet changes.

17. Americans like to eat red meat. In ________, many other cultures prefer to eat more fruit and vegetables.

18. I eat three pieces of fruit every day to stay healthy. ________, I eat four types of vegetables every day, too.

DOWN CLUES

1. I am ________. Which types of meat are not healthy to eat too much of?

2. ________ means every day.

4. ________, Sara does not have a healthy diet. I am worried about her.

6. Lee eats well and exercises every day. ________, he is quite healthy.

8. Eating healthy food helps ________ disease.

10. Fruit, vegetables, meat, and dairy are a few of the ________ food groups.

11. I know I need to eat healthy food such as fruit and vegetables. On the other ________, I really enjoy cake and cookies.

16. Some types of food, such as animal fat, can ________ disease.

UNIT **3**

Making a Difference

A rescued orphan elephant with her keeper

1. What do some people do to help other people?
2. What are some ways people can have less stress in their lives?

CHAPTER 5 Volunteer Vacations

Prereading

1. What are volunteers?

____

2. What kinds of work do volunteers do? Work in a small group. Use the diagram on the next page to help you organize your answers. When you are finished, share your answers with the class.

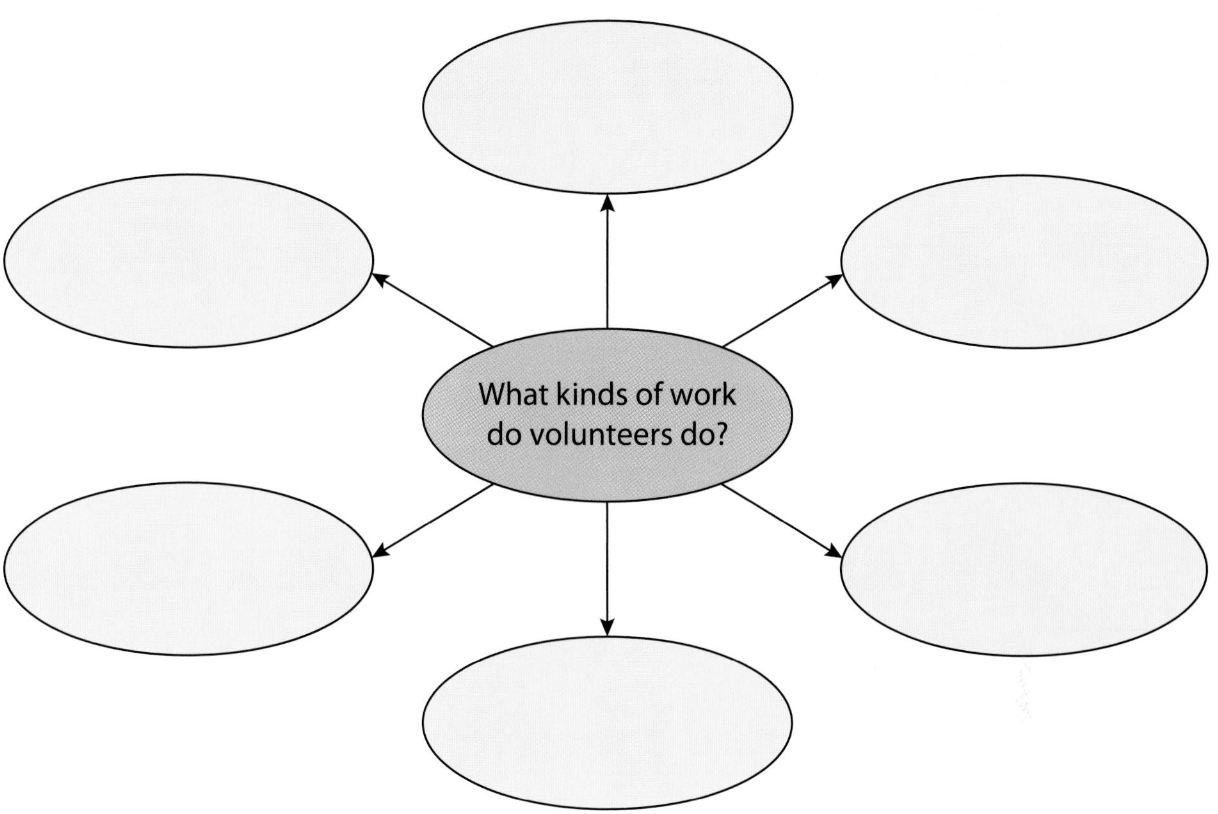

3. Look at the photo on page 72. What are these people doing?

____

4. Who do you think they are building the house for?

____

5. What are some reasons that people volunteer to help others?

____

Scientists and a volunteer in the Peruvian Amazon

Reading

CD 1
TR 10

Read the following passage carefully. Then complete the exercises that follow.

Volunteer Vacations

Everyone enjoys taking a vacation. A vacation is fun and relaxing. Some people like to go to the beach and swim. Other people go to the mountains or visit another country. Many other people use their vacation time for other reasons. What do they do? They take volunteer vacations to help other people. Volunteers are people who work but don't receive any money for it. They do this because they want to help other people. Many organizations give volunteers a chance to help others.

Habitat for Humanity is one of these organizations. Habitat for Humanity is an organization of volunteers who build homes for people in need. The most famous volunteer is former U.S. President Jimmy Carter, who won the Nobel Peace Prize. Habitat for Humanity volunteers don't need any special skills. They just need to be in good health. Volunteers build homes in the United States, but they also construct homes all over the world in places such as Honduras, Fiji, and Ethiopia. Volunteers pay for their own trips. For example, a two-week trip to Honduras, Indonesia, or Cambodia is about $1,900.

Another volunteer organization is called Earthwatch. Earthwatch gets many volunteers to help scientists do research in many places around the world. For example, volunteers may study endangered animals such as koala bears in Australia. Most of the trips are two weeks. Volunteers pay about $2,975 to participate, not including airfare. They usually stay in dormitories and make dinner together. Thousands of people work as volunteers with Earthwatch. The volunteers range in age from 10 to 80 years old!

Cross-Cultural Solutions is another volunteer organization. It helps communities in many countries, including Ghana, India, Peru, and Thailand. Cross-Cultural Solutions provides health care and education to many people. Twelve to eighteen volunteers work together for about three weeks at one location. The work depends on the volunteers' skills. For instance, if a volunteer has special medical training, he or she may work in a local hospital. Volunteers have evenings and two weekends to spend on their own. Prices begin at $3,000 for a two-week trip, not including airfare.

People who take volunteer vacations believe they are helping people around the world to live better lives. They believe they can help other people get an education or provide them with a better place to live. For the volunteers, this is the best vacation of all.

A volunteer with a koala in Australia

Fact Finding

Read the passage again. Then read the following statements. Check (√) whether each statement is True or False. If a statement is false, rewrite it so that it is true. Then go back to the passage and find the line that supports your answer.

1. _____ True _____ False Volunteer vacations are fun and relaxing.

____

2. _____ True _____ False Habitat for Humanity volunteers build houses all around the world.

____

3. _____ True _____ False Former U.S. President Jimmy Carter helps build houses for people in need.

____

4. _____ True _____ False Earthwatch helps doctors take care of people.

____

5. _____ True _____ False Cross-Cultural Solutions helps people with education.

____

6. _____ True _____ False All volunteer organizations pay the volunteers.

____

7. _____ True _____ False Volunteers pay for their own airfare.

____

8. _____ True _____ False Volunteer vacations are usually for only a week.

____

Reading Analysis

Read each question carefully. Circle the letter or the number of the correct answer.

1. **Volunteers** are people who work but don't receive any money for it. Habitat for Humanity is an organization of volunteers who build homes for **people in need**.

   a. **Volunteers** are people who
      1. work without pay.
      2. need other people.
      3. need some help.

   b. **People in need**
      1. want someone to do something for them.
      2. cannot always help themselves.
      3. volunteer to help others.

2. Many **organizations** give volunteers a chance to help others.
   An **organization** is

   a. a business that doesn't pay people for working.
   b. a group of people who work but do not ask for money.
   c. a group of people working together for a specific purpose.

3. The most famous volunteer is **former** U.S. President Jimmy Carter, who won the Nobel Peace Prize.

   Former means that Jimmy Carter

   a. was the U.S. president in the past but is not the U.S. president now.
   b. worked in the government but does not work there now.
   c. was very popular in the past but is not popular now.

4. Habitat for Humanity volunteers don't need any special **skills**. They just need to be in good health.

   A **skill** is

   a. the ability to speak a language well.
   b. the ability to do something well.
   c. the ability to build a home.

5. Volunteers build homes in the United States, but they also **construct** homes all over the world in places such as Honduras, Fiji, and Ethiopia.

   Construct means

   a. volunteer.
   b. help.
   c. build.

6. Earthwatch gets many volunteers to help scientists **do research** in places around the world. For example, volunteers may study **endangered** animals **such as** koala bears in Australia.
   a. **Do research** means
      1. to study something carefully.
      2. to do volunteer work.
      3. to travel to different places.
   b. **Endangered** animals are
      1. animals from other countries.
      2. animals that may disappear forever.
      3. dangerous animals.
   c. **Such as** means
      1. for example.
      2. also.
      3. however.

7. Volunteers pay about $2,975 to **participate**, not including **airfare**.
   a. **Participate** means
      1. to travel.
      2. to pay money.
      3. to be part of a group.
   b. **Airfare** is
      1. the name of the organization.
      2. the cost of an airplane ticket.
      3. the length of the trip.

8. Earthwatch volunteers usually stay in **dormitories** and make dinner together. **Dormitories** are
   a. individual homes.
   b. homes for groups of people.
   c. hotels.

9. **Volunteers range in age from 10 to 80 years old!** This sentence means that
   a. you must be 10 years old to volunteer.
   b. people of many different ages can volunteer.
   c. people who are older than 80 cannot volunteer.

10. Cross-Cultural Solutions **provides** health care and education to many people. **Provides** means
   a. discusses.
   b. understands.
   c. gives.

11. Twelve to eighteen volunteers work together for about three weeks at one **location**. A **location** is

a. a job.
b. a place.
c. a person.

12. For instance, if a volunteer has special **medical** training, he or she may work in a **local** hospital.

a. **Medical** knowledge means
   1. someone knows about volunteering.
   2. someone knows about medicine.
   3. someone has a special skill.

b. **Local** means
   1. far away.
   2. poor.
   3. nearby.

13. Prices **begin at** $3,000 for a **two-week** trip, **not including airfare**.

a. **Begin at** $3,000 means that
   1. $3,000 is the highest price.
   2. $3,000 is the usual price.
   3. $3,000 is the lowest price.

b. **Not including airfare** means
   1. you also need to buy your own airplane ticket.
   2. your airplane ticket is part of the cost.

c. A **two-week** trip
   1. will cost at least $3,000.
   2. will usually cost $3,000.
   3. will always cost $3,000.

14. What is the main idea of this passage?

a. Vacation volunteers receive money for helping people all around the world build their own homes.
b. Vacation volunteers work with organizations to help people around the world live better lives.
c. Vacation volunteers travel around the world to have fun and to relax in different countries.

Vocabulary Skills

PART 1

Recognizing Word Forms

In English, there are several ways that verbs change to nouns. Some verbs become nouns by adding the suffix *-tion,* for example, *collect (v.), collection (n.).* Some words change spelling, for example, *explain (v.), explanation (n.).*

Complete each sentence with the correct word form on the left. Write all the verbs in the simple present. The nouns may be singular or plural.

educate *(v.)* **education *(n.)***	**1.** Some volunteer groups provide __________ to people around the world. The volunteers __________ children in many countries.
locate *(v.)* **location *(n.)***	**2.** Volunteer organizations __________ communities that need help. The volunteers work in many different __________, such as the United States, Europe, and Asia.
construct *(v.)* **construction *(n.)***	**3.** The __________ of a new home can be very fast when many people work together. The volunteers __________ homes in many cities around the world.
organize *(v.)* **organization *(n.)***	**4.** When an __________ works well, it helps many people. Habitat for Humanity __________ workers to build houses for people in need.
solve *(v.)* **solution *(n.)***	**5.** Volunteer organizations __________ many different kinds of problems. These groups look for __________ to problems in education and health care for people in need.

PART 2

Recognizing Word Connections

Word connections are important. They can help you when you write and speak. For example, the verbs *have, do,* and *make* connect with many nouns.

Read the following sentences. Complete each sentence with the correct words from the box.

do/does homework	have/has fun	make/makes plans
do/does research	have/has knowledge	make/makes dinner

1. Are you busy tonight? I want to ____________________ with you to go out for dinner.
2. I think the library is the best place to ____________________.
3. I enjoy going to the cafeteria with my classmates. We always ____________________ when we eat together.
4. You can talk to your doctor about your medicine. He or she ____________________ about your health.
5. Scientists ____________________ on many different diseases. They want to learn how to prevent and cure them.
6. Sophia often ____________________ for her friends and family. She's a great cook!

Vocabulary in Context

Read the following sentences. Complete each sentence with the correct word from the box. Use each word only once.

construct *(v.)*	former *(adj.)*	research *(v.)*	vacation *(n.)*
dormitory *(n.)*	location *(n.)*	skill *(n.)*	volunteer *(n.)*

1. Kim is a university student. He lives in a ______________ on campus.
2. John is the ______________ president of the company. He stopped working here last year.
3. I work at a hospital after school. I'm a ______________, so I don't earn any money.
4. There are a lot of children in my city, so the government must ______________ more schools.
5. My mother is a very hard worker. She needs to take a ______________ so that she can relax.
6. New York is a beautiful city. I think it's a great ______________ for my next trip.
7. Justin is an excellent cook. He learned this ______________ from his grandmother.
8. I want to learn more about volunteer vacations. I will ______________ them online.

Reading Skill

Organizing Information in a Chart

It's important to be able to create charts. Charts can help you organize and understand information that you read.

Read the passage again. Use the information in the passage to complete the chart below.

	Habitat for Humanity	Earthwatch	Cross-Cultural Solutions
What do they do?			
Where do the volunteers work?			
How long are the volunteer vacations?			
How much does it cost?			
Other information			

Another Look

CD 1 TR 11

Read the following passage about people who do volunteer work. Then answer the questions that follow.

Who Volunteers?

People volunteer in order to help people in need. They also volunteer in order to "give back" to their community. This means that they want to assist the people in their community who need help. However, volunteering is not only good for the community and those in need, but it is good for the volunteers, too. Volunteer Canada, an organization in Canada, started National Volunteer Week in 1943. Today, it is still very popular. In fact, six million people around the country volunteer every year.

Who volunteers? All kinds of people volunteer. For example, senior citizens (people over 65 years old) volunteer for many reasons. They want to meet new friends and stay active. Senior citizens often have a lot of free time. They can use this time to help other people. Sometimes, when people graduate from college, they do volunteer work. Then they can get some skills and experience before they find a job. Other people volunteer because it gives them a chance to do something different. New immigrants to Canada also volunteer. By volunteering, they get work experience and can also improve their English and French language skills.

All of these volunteers in Canada do different kinds of work, but they have something in common: They are helping other people. And by doing this, they are helping themselves, too.

Volunteers construct a house.

QUESTIONS FOR ANOTHER LOOK

1. Who are **senior citizens**?
   a. Volunteers
   b. People over 65 years old
   c. College graduates

2. Who are **immigrants**?
   a. People who come from another country
   b. People who were born in Canada
   c. People who volunteer

3. Who started National Volunteer Week in Canada?

   ____

4. Look at the chart below. Why do these people volunteer? Write the reasons.

Volunteers	Why do they volunteer?
Senior citizens	
College graduates	
New immigrants	

Topics for Discussion and Writing

1. This chapter discusses three volunteer organizations. Which one do you think does the most important work? Why? Write your reasons and give examples.

2. Former U.S. President Jimmy Carter is very famous. Do you think it is a good idea for famous people to volunteer to help others? Why or why not? Explain your reasons.

3. What was your favorite vacation? Why? Who did you go with? Write about what you did on your favorite vacation.

4. Write in your journal. Will you ever volunteer to work with an organization such as Habitat for Humanity, Earthwatch, or Cross-Cultural Solutions? If so, which one? Why? If not, why not?

Critical Thinking

1. Work in a group. What can volunteers do for people in need? Make a list. Share your ideas with your classmates.

2. Work in pairs. Imagine you are going to interview the director of National Volunteer Week in Canada. Make a list of questions you want to ask this person. Compare your list of questions with those of your classmates.

3. Discuss this question with your classmates: Former U.S. President Jimmy Carter is a volunteer for Habitat for Humanity. Why do you think he volunteers to help build houses for people in need?

4. Why do so many people work hard to help people they do not know, in countries they do not live in? What do you think?

Crossword Puzzle

Review the words in the box below. Then read the clues on the next page. Write the words in the correct spaces in the puzzle.

airfare	endangered	medical	range
begin	former	need	research
construct	local	organization	skill
dormitories	location	participate	volunteer

Crossword Puzzle Clues

ACROSS CLUES

1. In a rural town, the __________ school is usually small.
5. Next year, I plan to __________ in a vacation where I help build a home.
9. The hospital needs people with __________ knowledge to help the doctors and nurses.
10. Workers stay in one __________ for about three weeks.
13. Prices for these special vacations __________ at $3,000, not including airfare.
14. People who work for special organizations __________ in age from 10 to 80 years old!
15. Scientists do __________ everywhere. They study all kinds of plants and animals.
16. People in __________ often don't have enough food and fresh water.

DOWN CLUES

2. Cross-Cultural Solutions is an __________ that helps people in many countries.
3. I have a special __________. I can fix machines, even old ones.
4. The __________ from New York to Cambodia is very expensive, and it is a long flight.
6. Many animals are __________. There are not many of them, and they may die out.
7. __________ often have several beds in one room.
8. A __________ is someone who offers to work but does not receive any pay.
11. Habitat for Humanity wants to __________ new homes for the poor next year.
12. The __________ governor of our state gave a speech about helping people in poor countries. She was governor from 2010 to 2014.

CHAPTER 6 Improving Lives with Pet Therapy

Prereading

Discuss these questions with a partner.

1. Look at the photo. Describe the man. How do you think he feels? Why do you think he feels this way?

2. Work with a partner and fill in the chart below. When you are finished, compare your responses with the rest of the class.

Problems	Solutions
What do you do when you feel lonely?	
What do you do when you feel stressed?	
What do you do when you are sick?	

3. Take a class survey. How many students like dogs? Why? How many students like cats? Why?

Number of Students Who Like Dogs: ______	Number of Students Who Like Cats: ______
Reasons:	Reasons:

4. There are approximately 68 million dogs in homes in the United States and approximately 73 million cats. Why do you think Americans have so many pets in their homes?

____

____

5. Read the title of this chapter. How can pets improve people's lives? Make a list.

______________________ ______________________

______________________ ______________________

Reading

CD 1
TR 12

Read the following passage carefully. Then complete the exercises that follow.

Improving Lives with Pet Therapy

Do you sometimes feel lonely? Do you sometimes feel stressed? Do you sometimes get sick? If you answered yes to these questions, you might not need a doctor. Instead, you might just need a pet. Pets, such as dogs, cats, or even birds, can make you feel better. In fact, many people feel healthier when they have a pet to take care of.

People who have pets often feel calmer and less lonely than people who don't have pets. For example, Juliet Locke has a six-year-old cat named Snowball. "Snowball knows when I'm having a bad day. When I'm sitting in a chair, she'll jump on my lap, and I'll pet her. She really helps me feel relaxed," says Juliet. Pets can help you have a healthy mind, and they can give you a healthy body, too. Dr. R.K. Anderson is a veterinarian. He started CENSHARE (Center to Study Human/Animal Relationships and Environments), an organization that researches how pets affect people. These researchers believe that people with pets are healthier than people without pets. For instance, pet owners often have lower rates of heart disease than people without pets. Many pet owners don't have high blood pressure either.

While most people think of dogs and cats as pets, having birds and fish can also be effective. In fact, people own many different kinds of pets. Researchers studied the effects of these kinds of animals on their owners' health. The researchers found that some people actually lower their blood pressure by watching fish in a tank or by listening to the sounds of birds. These activities are very calming.

Richard Waxman believes that all people should have the chance to spend time with a pet. He started a group called "Paws and Hearts." It is a volunteer organization that brings animals to nursing homes, hospitals, and senior centers. Mr. Waxman says that each patient can become friends with a loving dog. As a result, the patients feel calmer and also have less physical pain. This is called "pet therapy," and people love the animals' visits. For example, Clara Wu lives at a nursing home in Palm Desert, California. "I just love when the volunteers bring the dogs to visit us," Mrs. Wu says. "It brings back wonderful memories of other dogs I've owned." Mr. Waxman agrees. "Pet therapy allows for a great connection between the past and the present that can be very powerful."

Paws and Hearts isn't only for adults. The organization also has a reading program for children called "Paws to Read." Volunteers bring dogs to schools and libraries. There, children sit with the dogs and read stories to them. This activity often improves the children's reading skills as well as their self-confidence. Then, when they return to their classrooms, they feel more sure of themselves and can read aloud more easily and clearly. It's easy to see that pet therapy is useful for people of all ages.

A child reads to a dog from the group "Paws to Read."

Fact Finding

Read the passage again. Then read the following statements. Check (√) whether each statement is True or False. If a statement is false, rewrite it so that it is true. Then go back to the passage and find the line that supports your answer.

1. ____ True ____ False People who have pets often feel less healthy than people who don't have pets.

   ____

2. ____ True ____ False Snowball is a six-year-old dog.

   ____

3. ____ True ____ False People sometimes feel calm by watching fish in a tank or by listening to the sounds of birds.

   ____

4. ____ True ____ False Patients at a nursing home in Palm Desert, California, are happy when the pets come to visit them.

   ____

5. ____ True ____ False Volunteers from "Paws to Read" bring dogs to nursing homes and hospitals.

   ____

6. ____ True ____ False The children's reading skills often improve by reading stories to the dogs.

   ____

Reading Analysis

Read each question carefully. Circle the letter or the number of the correct answer, or write your answer in the space provided.

1. Do you sometimes feel lonely? Do you sometimes feel stressed? Do you sometimes get sick? If you answered yes to these questions, you might not need a doctor. **Instead**, you might just need a **pet**. Pets, such as dogs, cats, or even birds, can make you feel better. **In fact**, many people feel healthier when they have a pet to take care of.

   a. **Instead** means
      1. in place of.
      2. in addition to.
      3. together with.

   b. A **pet** is
      1. an animal you keep in your home.
      2. a dog or a cat.
      3. a bird.

   c. Which animals can make you feel better?
      1. Only dogs and cats
      2. Only birds
      3. Dogs, cats, birds, and other animals

   d. What kind of information follows **in fact**?
      1. New, different information from the idea in the previous sentence
      2. More details about the idea in the previous sentence
      3. An example of the idea in the previous sentence

2. People who have pets often feel **calmer** and less lonely than people who don't have pets. **Calm** means
   a. lonely.
   b. peaceful.
   c. sick.

3. "Snowball knows when I'm having **a bad day**. When I'm sitting in a chair, she'll jump on my **lap**, and I'll pet her. She really helps me feel **relaxed**," says Juliet.

   a. **A bad day** means
      1. an unhappy or stressful day.
      2. a day with bad weather.
      3. an unlucky day.

   b. Someone's **lap** is
      1. the chair a person is sitting on.
      2. the top of your legs when you are sitting down.
      3. a small table.

c. When you feel **relaxed**, you feel
   1. calm.
   2. tired.
   3. sleepy.

4. Pets can help you have a healthy **mind**, and they can give you a healthy body, too. Your **mind** is

a. the part of you that exercises.
b. the part of you that sees.
c. the part of you that thinks and remembers.

5. Dr. R.K. Anderson is a **veterinarian**. He started the Center to Study Human/Animal Relationships and **Environments**.

a. A **veterinarian** is
   1. a doctor who cares for people's bodies.
   2. a doctor who cares for people's minds.
   3. a doctor who cares for animals.

b. Your **environment** is
   1. everything around you.
   2. the pet you have.
   3. the relationship you have.

6. These researchers believe that people with pets are healthier than people without pets. **For instance**, pet owners often have lower rates of heart disease than people without pets. Many **pet owners** don't have high blood pressure either.

While most people think of dogs and cats as pets, birds and fish can also be effective. In fact, people own many different kinds of pets.

a. **For instance** means
   1. however.
   2. for example.
   3. of course.

b. A **pet owner** is someone who
   1. has a pet at home.
   2. likes animals.
   3. has high blood pressure.

c. How are people with pets healthier than people without pets?
   1. They often have lower rates of heart disease.
   2. They typically don't have high blood pressure.
   3. Both 1 and 2

d. Which animals can help improve people's lives?
   1. Dogs
   2. Cats
   3. Birds
   4. Fish
   5. All of the above

7. Researchers studied the **effects** of these animals on their owners' health.
Effects means
   a. places.
   b. results.
   c. causes.

8. Volunteers bring dogs to schools and libraries. **There**, children sit with the dogs and read stories to them. This activity helps to improve the children's reading skills as well as their **self-confidence**. Then, when they return to their classrooms, they feel more sure of themselves and can read **aloud** more easily and clearly.
   a. **There** refers to
      1. in schools and libraries.
      2. only in schools.
      3. only in libraries.
   b. When you read **aloud**, you read
      1. silently, without speaking.
      2. quietly to yourself.
      3. so that others can hear you.
   c. What group of words in these sentences is a synonym for **self-confidence**?

      ____

9. What is the main idea of this reading?
   a. People in hospitals feel healthier when pets visit them.
   b. Pets can be very helpful to people.
   c. People of all ages enjoy pets.

Vocabulary Skills

PART 1

Recognizing Word Forms

In English, some nouns become adjectives by adding the suffix *-ful*, for example, *hope (n.), hopeful (adj.).*

Complete each sentence with the correct word form on the left. The nouns are all singular.

stress *(n.)* **1.** It can be very ____________ to be in a hospital. Patients feel

stressful *(adj.)* a lot of ____________ because they are sick.

pain ***(n.)***	**2.**	Patients in hospitals have less ______________ when dogs come to visit.
painful ***(adj.)***		Some illnesses can be very ______________.
help ***(n.)***	**3.**	Dogs and cats are very ______________ for pet therapy. People in nursing
helpful ***(adj.)***		homes enjoy the ______________ from these animals.
power ***(n.)***	**4.**	The pets from Paws to Read have a ______________ effect on the young students.
powerful ***(adj.)***		The dogs give children the ______________ to read with confidence.
use ***(n.)***	**5.**	The ______________ of pets in therapy is a great idea for everyone. The pets
useful (adj.)		can be ______________ for children and adults, too.

PART 2

Recognizing Word Connections: Prepositions That Follow Verbs

Prepositions follow certain verbs in English. Verb and preposition combinations can help you when you write and speak. For example, *take care of, think of, spend time with, improve with, listen to,* and *return to* are common verb and preposition combinations.

Read the following sentences. Complete each sentence with the correct words from the box.

improve with	return to	take care of
listen to	spend time with	think of

1. I always ______________________ my friends on the weekends. We usually have a lot of fun together.
2. We ______________________ our teacher carefully when she explains the lessons.
3. Our English skills ______________________ help from our teachers.
4. After lunch, the students ______________________ the classroom to continue their studies.
5. Jane and Susan ______________________ their grandfather every evening. He is very ill and needs their help.
6. We usually ______________________ only dogs and cats as pets, but many people have other kinds of pets, such as birds and fish.

Vocabulary in Context

Read the following sentences. Complete each sentence with the correct word or phrase from the box. Use each word or phrase only once.

aloud *(adv.)*	for instance	powerful *(adj.)*	stressful *(adj.)*
effective *(adj.)*	instead *(adv.)*	self-confidence *(n.)*	therapy *(n.)*

1. Our teacher sometimes reads ______________________ to us in class. We always listen carefully and take notes.

2. Marina enjoys reading as much as she can. ______________________, she reads on the bus, during lunch, and before class, too.

3. I wanted a dog for a pet, but my parents said no, so I got a cat ______________________.

4. My classmates and I help each other when we do our homework together. It's more ______________________ than doing it alone.

5. Sung Min plays the piano very well. He has a lot of ______________________ and is never afraid to perform for large groups of people.

6. Having a pet, listening to soft music, and taking a warm bath are all very effective kinds of ______________________. They all help us feel relaxed.

7. The first day of school can be ______________________. However, students often feel calmer after the first week.

8. Doctors can give patients very ______________________ medicine for pain when aspirin isn't strong enough.

Reading Skill

Understanding a Pie Chart

Pie charts contain important information about a topic. They show percentages or parts of a whole.

Look at the pie charts and read the sentences. Put a check (√) next to the sentences that are true.

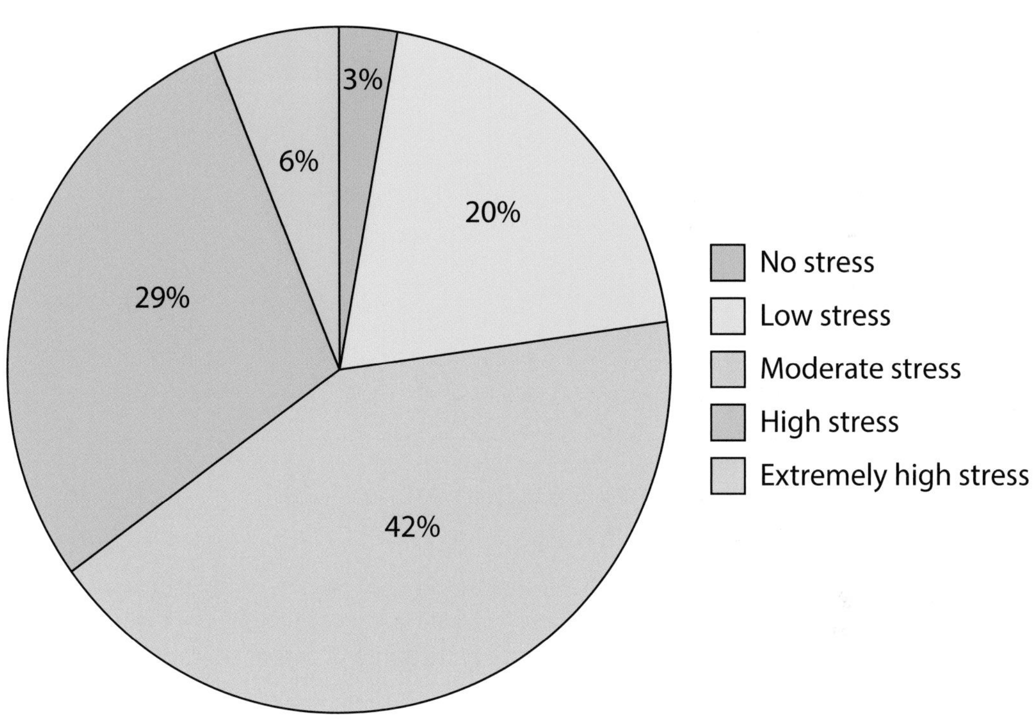

1. _____ Most students have low levels of stress.

2. _____ Almost half of the students have moderate levels of stress.

3. _____ More students have high levels of stress than low levels of stress.

4. _____ All students have some stress.

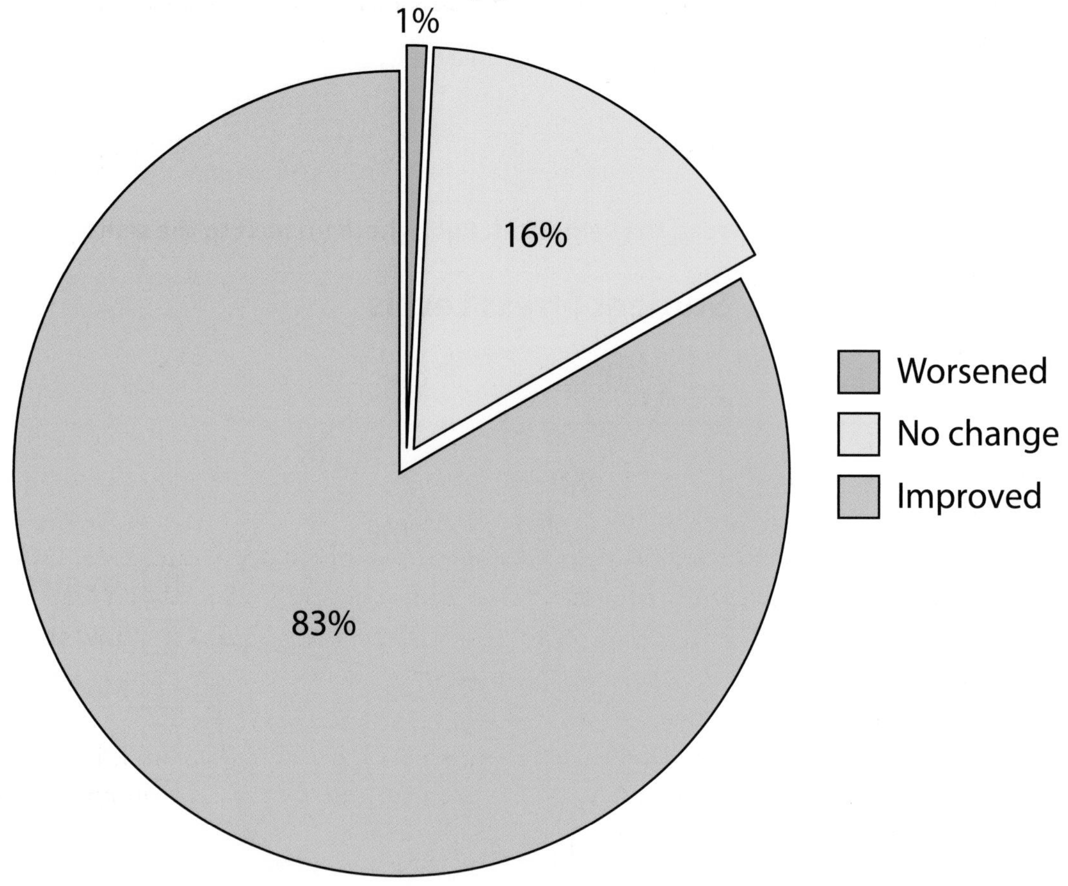

5. ____ Stress levels improved for most students after pet therapy.

6. ____ Stress levels didn't improve for most students after pet therapy.

7. ____ Stress levels improved for all students after pet therapy.

8. ____ Stress levels didn't change for some students after pet therapy.

Another Look

 CD 1 TR 13 **Read the following story about pet therapy at a university. Then answer the questions that follow.**

A New Way to Relieve Student Stress

It's the last week of the semester at the University of Wisconsin. The students are preparing for their final exams. Of course, this is a very stressful week for many of them. Some are at the library, but they are not studying. Instead, they are sitting and relaxing with dogs, but they are not wasting their time.

The Health Department of the university brings the dogs to the school library for the students. The dogs help them reduce stress as they prepare for their finals. Counselors from the school bring the dogs, but they also give advice to students about how to feel less anxious. They advise students to take short study breaks—even five minutes every hour—to reduce stress. These frequent breaks also help students remember information. In addition, the counselors advise students to get enough sleep. "Don't drink a lot of coffee because that will prevent you from sleeping," one counselor suggests. "Try not to worry so much," another counselor says, "and ask your friends and family for their assistance."

Manuel Perez, a University of Wisconsin student, says that all of the advice is very useful. However, he says, "The dogs are the most useful of all. When I'm petting one, I feel much more relaxed, and then I'm ready to hit the books."

Students relax and play with dogs in a college library.

QUESTIONS FOR ANOTHER LOOK

1. Why is this a stressful week for the students?

____

2. How do the dogs help the students?

____

3. What advice did the counselor give the students to feel less stress?

a. ____

b. ____

c. ____

4. "I'm ready to **hit the books**."
Hit the books is an idiom. It means

a. study.
b. quit school.
c. take an exam.

Topics for Discussion and Writing

1. Do you have a pet? If so, describe it. Explain why you enjoy your pet. If you don't have a pet, do you want to get one? Why or why not? Explain your answer.

2. How do you relax when you feel stressed? What helps you relax? Write about it.

3. The reading talks about cats, dogs, birds, and fish as helpful pets. Which animal could be most effective for certain people? For example, which animal might be most helpful for a child? For an elderly person? For someone in a hospital?

4. The reading talks about the usefulness of pets for the elderly and for children. What other people can pets help? How can they be helpful?

5. Write in your journal. Write about a time when you felt a lot of stress. Why was this situation stressful? Give examples.

Critical Thinking

1. Read the following statistics about cats and dogs. Then read the sentences that follow. Fill in the blanks with the words *cat* or *dog*.

Dogs

- There are approximately 68 million dogs in homes in the United States.
- Four in ten (or 40 million) U.S. households own at least one dog.
- Most dog owners own one dog (63%).
- About one-fourth (24%) of dog owners own two dogs.
- On average, dog owners spend about $200 per year on veterinary-related expenses.

Cats

- There are approximately 73 million cats in homes in the United States.
- Three in ten (or 34.7 million) U.S. households own at least one cat.
- One-half of cat owners (49%) own one cat; the remaining (51%) own two or more.
- On average, cat owners spend over $100 a year on veterinary-related expenses.

a. There are more __________ owners than __________ owners in the United States.

b. __________ owners spend more money on veterinary expenses than __________ owners.

c. Most __________ owners have more than one __________.

d. Most __________ owners have only one __________.

2. Work alone or with a partner. Choose a pet you want to have. Find out what the pet needs, such as food, exercise, a place to sleep, training, etc. How much will it cost to take care of this pet?

3. Why do you think people who have pets often feel calmer and less lonely than people who don't have pets? Discuss this question with your classmates.

4. Researchers say that pet owners often have lower rates of heart disease. Many pet owners don't have high blood pressure either. What do you think are reasons for this? Discuss your ideas with a partner.

Crossword Puzzle

Review the words in the box below. Then read the clues on the next page. Write the words in the correct spaces in the puzzle.

aloud	environment	lap	relaxed
calm	fact	mind	therapy
confidence	instance	owner	veterinarian
effects	instead	pet	

Crossword Puzzle Clues

ACROSS CLUES

3. Research shows that having a pet helps a person's self-__________.

6. Everything around us is our __________.

7. The __________ of something are its results.

10. I feel very __________ and peaceful when I pet my cat.

12. Many people use pet __________ to treat diseases of the body and the mind.

13. When I speak, I say something __________.

14. Many people feel better when they pet a cat or dog. In __________, 83 percent of people feel much better.

15. When Kim walks her dog in the park, she becomes very __________.

DOWN CLUES

1. A __________ is an animal doctor.

2. Anna doesn't have a __________. She cannot have any animals in her apartment.

4. That dog seems to be lost. Where is its __________? Who does it belong to?

5. My friend wanted a cat, but got a dog __________.

8. People like all kinds of pets. For __________, I like cats, my sister likes dogs, and my brother likes fish.

9. When I come home and sit down, my cat likes to sit on my __________.

11. We need a healthy body and a healthy __________.

UNIT **4**

Technology Today and Tomorrow

A *Robobee* sits on top of a flower. Robobees are tiny flying robots. Robert Wood is leading the development of Robobees at Harvard University's Microrobotics Lab. In the future, Robobees could help with search and rescue missions and gathering scientific data.

1. What are some ways technology can help us in our everyday lives?
2. How can doctors use technology to help people?

CHAPTER 7 Robots: The Face of the Future

An ASIMO robot in Tokyo

Prereading

Discuss these questions with a partner.

1. Look at the photo. This is a robot called ASIMO. What do you think it can do? Make a list.

_______________ _______________

_______________ _______________

2. ASIMO looks like a person. Do you think all robots look like people? __________

3. Where do people use robots? Circle your answers. You can choose more than one answer.
   a. At home
   b. At work
   c. At school

4. Did you ever see a robot? Where did you see it? What did it do?

5. Imagine you have a robot. What do you want the robot to do for you? Make a list.

   ______________________ ______________________

   ______________________ ______________________

Reading

Read the following passage carefully. Then complete the exercises that follow.

CD 1
TR 14

Robots: The Face of the Future

ASIMO traveled to Edinburgh, Scotland, for the annual Edinburgh International Science Festival. The festival takes place in February every year. Thousands of people came to visit the festival, but most of them came to see ASIMO. ASIMO is very famous because ASIMO is a robot. It is designed to run, climb stairs, and kick a soccer ball. It can even conduct an orchestra. In fact, when Yo Yo Ma, the famous cellist, performed at a concert in Detroit, Michigan, ASIMO was the conductor. Everyone at the concert was amazed not only by Yo Yo Ma, but also by ASIMO.

A robot is not a new idea. Scientists developed robots more than 60 years ago. For many years, robots have worked in factories. They do uninteresting jobs, such as packaging food or assembling cars. They are often used to do dangerous work as well. Most of these robots are shaped like machines; they do not look like people. However, ASIMO looks like a person. In addition, it is equipped with the ability to recognize and remember people.

While many countries are developing robots, Japan has the most robots of all. It is also developing more robots very quickly. In Japan, 20 percent of the people are over 65 years old. This means that a lot of Japanese people are senior citizens who no longer work. When people retire, robots can do their work. They can take care of the senior citizens, too. Japan hopes to have one million robots working in the country by the year 2025. A single robot can replace, or do the work of, ten people!

In the future, robots will become more useful and popular. Right now you can't buy a robot to do all your work, but you can buy one to help you around the house. A few years ago, iRobot, an American company, announced that it has robots that can wash, sweep, or vacuum your floors. Although these robots do not look like people, they can work just as hard!

A robot helps a woman in a grocery store.

Fact Finding

Read the passage again. Then read the following statements. Check (√) whether each statement is True or False. If a statement is false, rewrite it so that it is true. Then go back to the passage and find the line that supports your answer.

1. ____ True ____ False ASIMO can play the cello.

   ____

2. ____ True ____ False Some robots do uninteresting and dangerous jobs.

   ____

3. ____ True ____ False Most robots look like people.

   ____

4. ____ True ____ False ASIMO has the ability to recognize people.

   ____

5. ____ True ____ False Most people in Japan cannot work.

   ____

6. ____ True ____ False One robot can do the work of ten people.

   ____

7. ____ True ____ False Now you can buy a robot to clean your floors.

   ____

Reading Analysis

Read each question carefully. Circle the letter or the number of the correct answer.

1. ASIMO traveled to Edinburgh, Scotland, for the **annual** Edinburgh International Science Festival. The festival takes place in February every year.
   Annual means
   a. scientific.
   b. international.
   c. every year.

2. ASIMO is **designed** to run, climb stairs, and kick a soccer ball. It can even **conduct** an orchestra.

a. **Designed** means
   1. made.
   2. performed.
   3. climbed.

b. **Conduct** means
   1. play.
   2. lead.
   3. perform.

3. Everyone at the concert was **amazed not only** by Yo Yo Ma, **but also** by ASIMO.

a. **Amazed** means
   1. confused.
   2. surprised.
   3. interested.

b. **Not only . . . but also** means
   1. however.
   2. except.
   3. and.

c. Why were the people amazed by ASIMO?
   1. It's a good conductor.
   2. It can play the cello.
   3. It's a robot.

4. Scientists **developed** robots more than 60 years ago. For many years, robots have worked in factories. They do **uninteresting** jobs such as **packaging** food or **assembling** cars.

a. **Developed** means
   1. learned about.
   2. thought about.
   3. made.

b. Something **uninteresting** is
   1. dangerous.
   2. boring.
   3. difficult.

c. **Packaging** food is
   1. making food for a company.
   2. carrying food to a truck.
   3. putting food into boxes.

d. **Assembling** means
   1. putting together.
   2. driving.
   3. checking.

5. Most of these robots are **shaped like** machines; they do not look like people. However, ASIMO looks like a person. In addition, it is **equipped with** the ability to recognize and remember people.

a. **Shaped like** means
   1. to have the same form.
   2. to be the same size.

b. Which one of these is shaped like an egg? Circle your answer.
   1.
   2.
   3.

c. **Equipped with** means
   1. needs.
   2. makes.
   3. has.

6. In Japan, 20 percent of the people are over 65 years old. This means that a lot of Japanese people are **senior citizens** who no longer work.
Senior citizens are people who

a. do not work.
b. are 65 years old or older.
c. have important jobs.

7. Japan hopes to have one million robots working in the country by the year 2025. Does Japan have one million robots now?

a. Yes
b. No

8. A **single** robot can **replace**, or do the work of, ten people!

a. In this sentence, **single** means
   1. not married.
   2. only one.
   3. new.

b. In this sentence, **replace** means
   1. one robot equals ten people at work.
   2. ten robots equal one person at work.
   3. one robot equals one person at work.

9. In the future, robots will become more useful and **popular**.
Popular means

a. many people like it.
b. many people make it.
c. many people need it.

10. A few years ago, iRobot, an American company, **announced** that it has robots that can wash, sweep, or vacuum your floors.

Announced means

a. discovered.
b. said.
c. promised.

11. These robots do not look like people, but they can work **just as hard**!
This sentence means

a. robots can work harder than people.
b. people can work harder than robots.
c. robots can do the same work as people.

12. What is the main idea of this reading?

a. In the future, robots will do a lot of work for people.
b. Twenty percent of the people in Japan are senior citizens.
c. ASIMO can teach students and conduct an orchestra.

Vocabulary Skills

PART 1

Recognizing Word Forms

In English, some verbs become nouns by adding the suffix *-ment*, for example, *govern (v.), government (n.)*.

Complete each sentence with the correct word form on the left. Write all of the verbs in the past. The verbs may be affirmative or negative. The nouns may be singular or plural.

amaze *(v.)*
amazement *(n.)*

1. The people watched in ____________________ when ASIMO conducted the orchestra. ASIMO ____________________ the audience because the robot was the conductor!

develop *(v.)*
development *(n.)*

2. Many other companies ____________________ new robot technology last year. These technological ____________________ are happening more and more quickly.

equip ***(v.)*** **3.** Factories need heavy ____________ to assemble cars. Many car
equipment ***(n.)*** companies ____________ their factories with robots to do the heavy work years ago.

replace ***(v.)*** **4.** Fifty years ago, robots ____________ people at home, but they
replacement ***(n.)*** did in factories. Today, the ____________ of people by robots at home for housework is becoming more common.

announce ***(v.)*** **5.** iRobot made an important ____________ a few years ago.
announcement ***(n.)*** The company ____________ the development of Roomba, the robot that can clean floors.

PART 2

Recognizing Connecting Words

And, ***too***, ***as well***, ***also***, and ***in addition*** all have the same meaning. They connect ideas, but they are used differently in sentences.

a. Look back at the passage. Put the correct adverb in each sentence.

1. ASIMO looks like a person. ____________, it is equipped with the ability to recognize and remember people.
2. Robots will become more useful ____________ popular in the future.
3. Japan has the most robots of all. It is ____________ developing more robots very quickly.
4. Robots can do their work and help take care of the senior citizens, ____________.
5. Robots do boring work. They are often used to do dangerous work ____________.

b. Answer the questions below. Write the correct adverb(s).

1. Which two adverbs are at the end of a sentence? ____________ ____________
2. Which adverb is between two adjectives? ____________
3. Which adverb comes before a verb? ____________
4. Which adverb comes at the beginning of a sentence? ____________

Vocabulary in Context

Read the following sentences. Complete each sentence with the correct word or phrase from the box. Use each word or phrase only once.

amazed *(adj.)*	assemble *(v.)*	equipped *(adj.)*	replace *(v.)*
announced *(v.)*	design *(v.)*	recognize *(v.)*	senior citizens *(n.)*

1. The teacher ____________ that we are going to have a grammar test next week. I am going to begin studying this weekend.
2. My cell phone is broken. I'm going to return it to the store, and the store will ____________ it. I hope the new cell phone works better than this one!
3. Ann's new computer is ____________ with a DVD player, speakers, and a camera.
4. Mickey bought a new bookcase. He needs to ____________ it before he can use it.
5. My brother has a new haircut and looks very different. I almost didn't ____________ him!
6. Clara is learning English very quickly. She is ____________ at her fast progress.
7. Maryann really likes fashion, especially new clothes and shoes. She hopes to learn to ____________ clothing in college.
8. Many ____________ don't have to work any longer, so they have more time to spend with their grandchildren.

Reading Skill

Understanding a Pie Chart

Pie charts show percentages or parts of a whole. They show important information about a topic. Learning to read a pie chart can help you understand ideas from a reading passage.

a. Look at the pie chart and read the sentences below. Put a check (√) next to the sentences that are true.

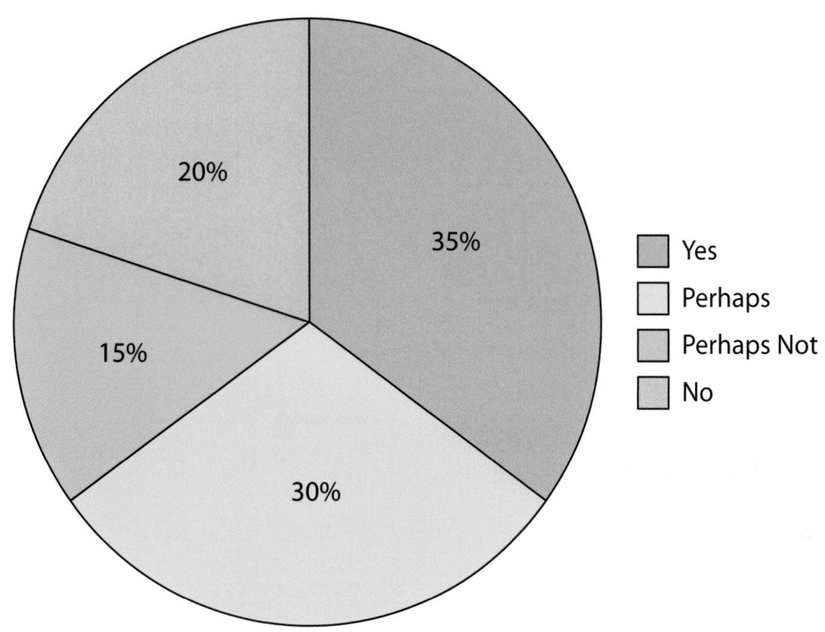

Source: http://whatjapanthinks.com/tag/robot/

1. ________ Everyone wants a robot to take care of them.

2. ________ Many people want a robot to take care of them.

3. ________ Most people don't want a robot to take care of them.

4. ________ Some people are not sure if they want a robot to take care of them.

b. Look at the pie chart below. Put a check (√) in the correct boxes.

Will personal care robots isolate seniors even more? Or will they help seniors to socialize better?

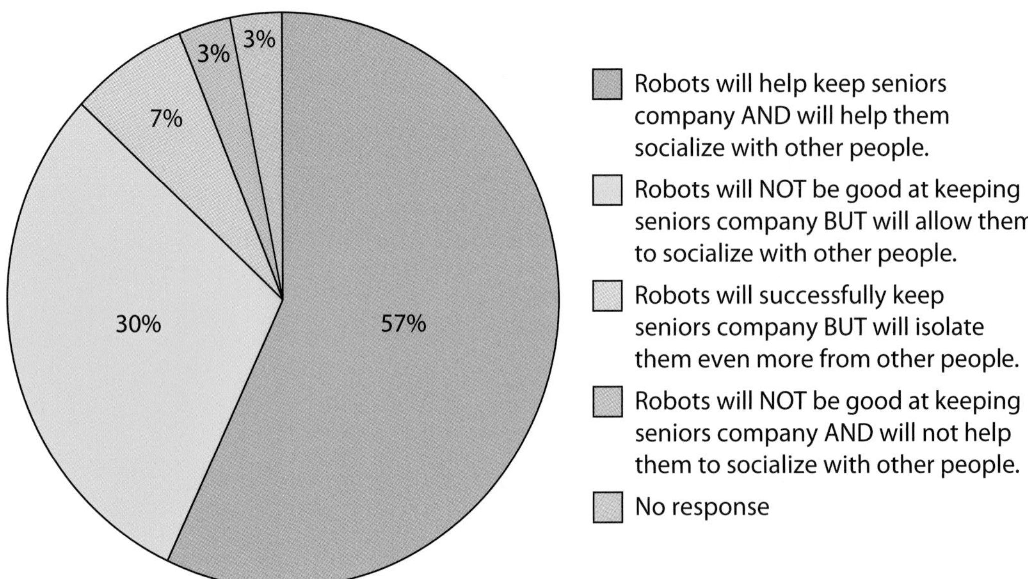

Source: http://www.openroboethics.org/results-robots-will-enable-seniors-to-socialize-more-says-readers/

	Robots will help keep seniors company.		Robots will allow seniors to socialize with other people.	
	Yes	No	Yes	No
57% of people believe …				
30% of people believe …				
7% of people believe …				
3% of people believe …				

Another Look

CD 2 TR 2 **Read the following passage about a new teacher in Japan. Then answer the questions that follow.**

An Unusual Teacher

Yuki Ishito's new sixth-grade teacher, Sava, is like most teachers in Japan. This morning, she is calling the attendance list and asking the students in the back of the room to please be quiet. Sava smiles at the students and looks happy. "Thank you," she says. Sometimes she looks sad or angry. Other times, she can look surprised or scared. Sava doesn't really look different from Yuki's other teachers, but she is. Sava is a robot.

Hiroshi Kobayashi is a professor at the Tokyo University of Science. He developed Sava. "Robots that look like people are a big hit with young children," he said. Of course, Sava cannot really teach the students. She is remote controlled by a person through a camera inside the robot.

Japan and other countries hope that in the future robots will do a lot of the work that people do today. However, some scientists don't believe that a robot can replace a teacher. Professor Kobayashi says, "Sava is just meant to help people. The robot has no intelligence. It has no ability to learn. It's just a tool." Although Sava is not ready to be a real teacher, the children enjoy her visits.

A robot named Sava speaks to elementary school students in Tokyo.

QUESTIONS FOR ANOTHER LOOK

1. What can Sava do? Write three things.

   ____

   ____

   ____

2. "Robots that look like people are **a big hit** with young children."
   A big hit is an idiom. What does it mean?
   a. Famous
   b. Popular
   c. Effective

3. Do you think robots can replace teachers in the future? Why or why not?

   ____

   ____

   ____

Topics for Discussion and Writing

1. Robots can do many different jobs. What jobs do you think robots cannot do? Why not? Discuss your ideas with your classmates.
2. Robots do many dangerous and boring jobs. Robots also do interesting jobs. For example, ASIMO can conduct an orchestra. Will people be happy if robots do interesting jobs for them? Why or why not?
3. What are some of the advantages of having robots work in factories and other places, such as hospitals and homes for senior citizens? What are some of the disadvantages?
4. Write in your journal. Imagine that you have a robot teacher. Write a letter to a friend, and describe your robot teacher. Tell your friend about your class. Do you enjoy your robot teacher? Why or why not?

Critical Thinking

1. Work with a partner and design a new robot. What will it look like? What can it do?
2. Work in a small group. Pretend that you are the parents of children in a school. The school wants to replace a real teacher with a robot. You do not want your children to have a robot for a teacher. Give reasons why you think having a robot teacher is a bad idea.
3. Work in a small group. Pretend that you are the parents of children in a school. The school wants to replace a real teacher with a robot. You agree with this plan. Give reasons why you think having a robot teacher is a good idea.
4. Work in a small group. You manufacture robots that can teach children. Design an advertisement for your robot.
5. Discuss these questions with a partner. Most robots look like machines. They do not look like people. Is it important for robots to look like people? What do you think?
6. There are many senior citizens in Japan. In the future, robots will do their work and take care of them, too. How can robots take care of senior citizens? Talk about your ideas with your classmates.
7. In many countries, including Japan, people must retire, or stop working, by a certain age, usually when they are 60 or 65 years old. This is a law. What is the reason for this law? Discuss this with your class.
8. iRobot has robots that can wash, sweep, and vacuum. What else do you want a robot to do for you in your home? Make a list and then compare your list with your classmates' lists.

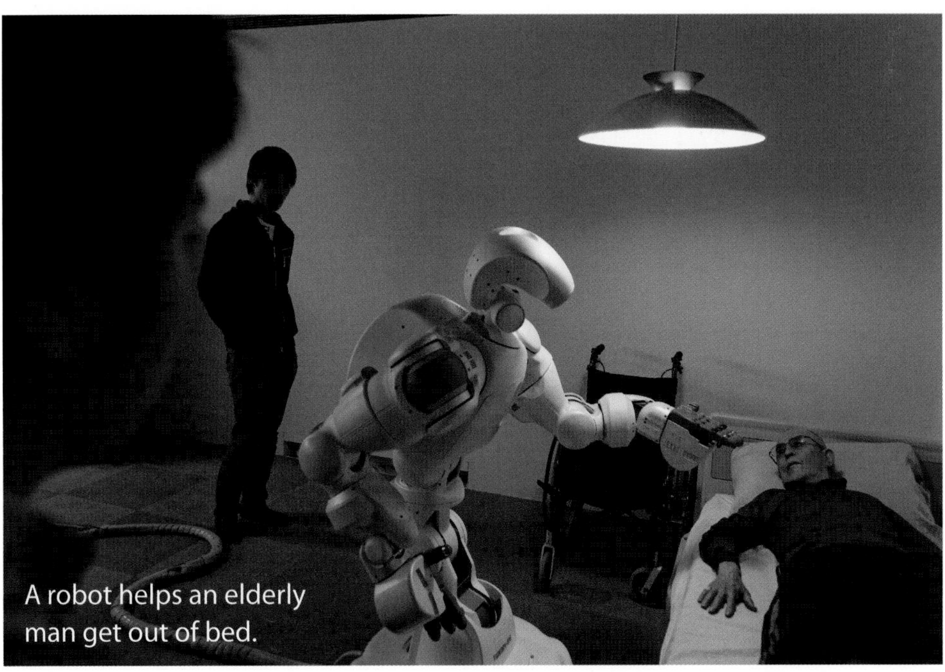
A robot helps an elderly man get out of bed.

Crossword Puzzle

Review the words in the box. Then read the clues on the next page. Write the words in the correct spaces in the puzzle.

amazed	conduct	packaging	shape
announce	designed	popular	single
annual	develop	replace	uninteresting
assemble	equip	senior	

1 2 3 4 5 6 7 8 9 10 11 12 13 14 15

Crossword Puzzle Clues

ACROSS CLUES

2. It takes a lot of experience to __________ an orchestra.
4. __________ means very surprised.
5. Will you __________ this robot with the ability to speak?
8. We need to __________ technology to help older people be independent.
9. One day, robots will have a more human __________. Now they look like machines.
10. A robot can never __________ a person in every way.
12. A 65-year-old person is a __________ citizen.
13. Automobile factories __________ thousands of cars every year.
14. A person's birthday is an __________ event.
15. The company will __________ the name of the new type of robot tomorrow.

DOWN CLUES

1. My car is __________ to save on gasoline.
3. I have a very __________ job. It is very boring.
6. People like the __________ on products to be colorful and easy to read.
7. ASIMO is a very __________ robot. Many people like it.
11. A __________ robot can do the work of ten people!

CHAPTER 8 A blind man sees again!

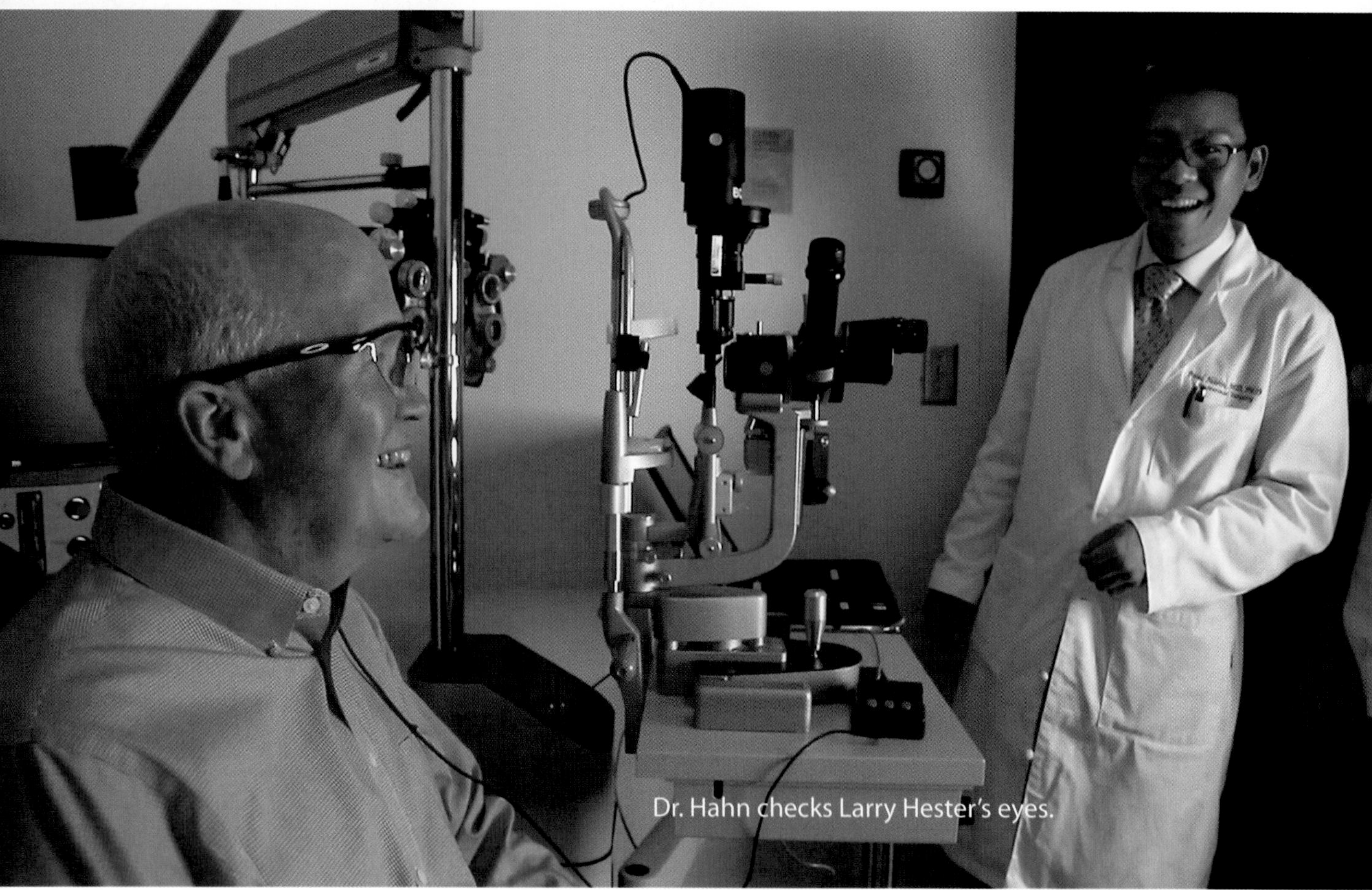
Dr. Hahn checks Larry Hester's eyes.

Prereading

1. Look at the photo. Where is this man?

a. In a movie theater
b. In an eye doctor's office
c. In a dentist's office

2. Look at the title of this chapter. Which sentence below best describes this man?

a. He has problems with his eyes and needs to wear glasses.
b. He was always blind, but now he can see.
c. He became blind a long time ago, but now he can see again.

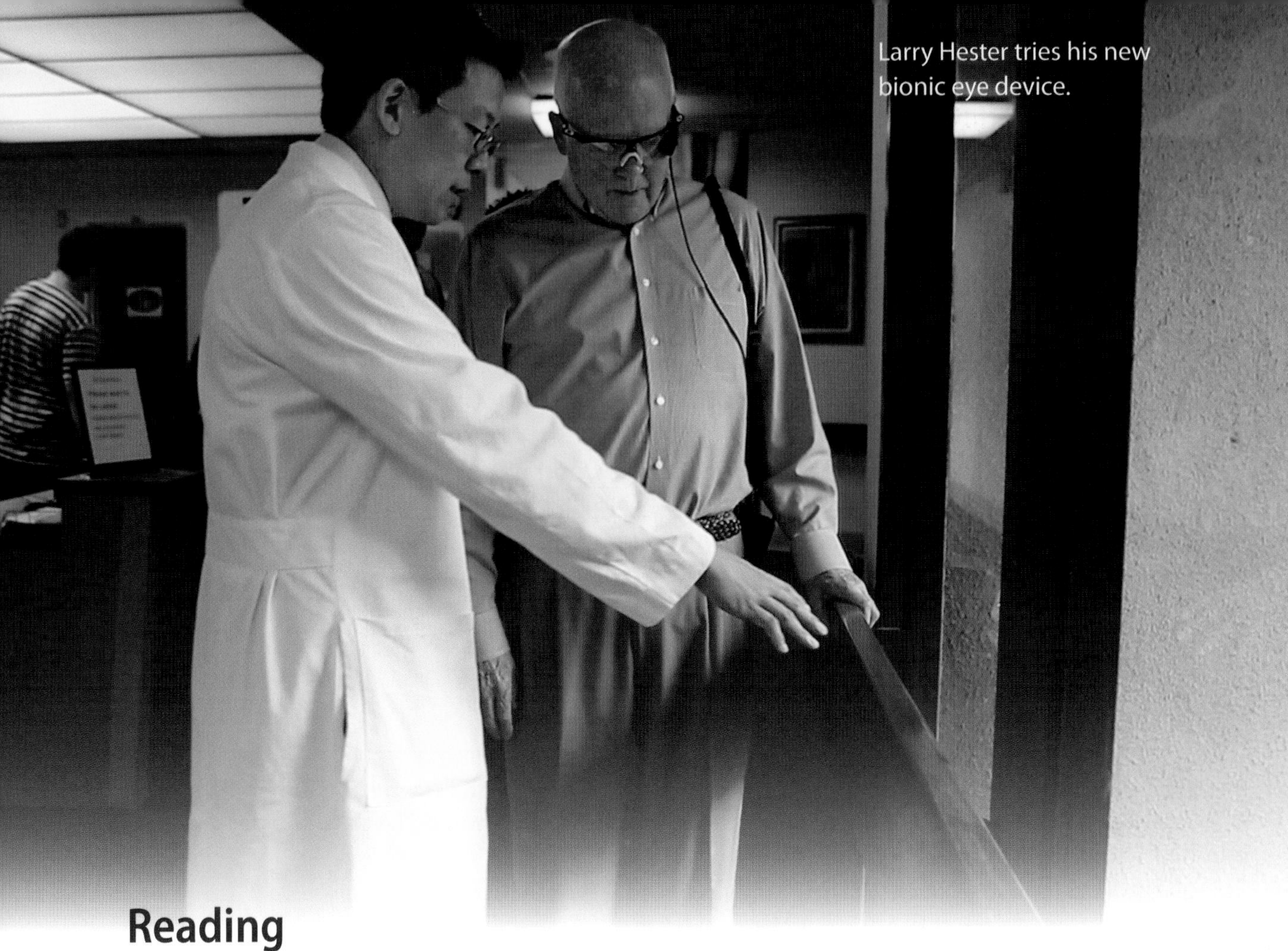

Larry Hester tries his new bionic eye device.

Reading

Read the following passage carefully. Then complete the exercises that follow.

CD 2
TR 3

A blind man sees again!

When Larry Hester was a young man, he started to have a problem with his eyes. He went to see many doctors. The doctors told him that he had a serious eye disease. The part of his eyes that sees light, the retina, was very weak. The doctors could not help Larry. His retina slowly became weaker. Eventually, Larry became blind. Although he lived in darkness for a very long time, Larry's life didn't stop. He used his memory to help him get around at home and at work, but it was not easy. Now, after 30 years, Larry can see again. How did this happen?

One day, Jenny, Larry's wife, read a story about a new device that might help her husband. Researchers at the Duke Eye Center in North Carolina developed a bionic, or robotic, eye. This device is a replacement for the retina, the part of the eye that responds to light. The weakness of the retina in Larry's eyes caused his blindness. The Hesters met with Dr. Paul Hahn, an eye surgeon from the Duke Eye Center.

He believed that he could help Larry. Dr. Hahn placed one of these devices in each of Larry's eyes. Then Dr. Hahn gave Larry a special pair of glasses. The glasses are connected to the device. At that moment, Larry saw light for the first time in 30 years. Larry took a deep breath. He was unable to describe his feelings, but he was very excited.

Larry is not the first person to receive this special device. There are other people who are blind for the same reason as Larry. But even with the device, these people cannot see objects clearly. The bionic eye is very simple. Larry's special glasses contain a tiny camera. The bionic eye picks up light signals from the camera. Larry, and others who have the same device, can only see light and shapes. However, this is amazing to people who could only see darkness. Perhaps in the future the technology will improve even more. Then people like Larry will be able to see much more. For Larry and other people like him, that will truly be an amazing day.

Fact Finding

Read the passage again. Then read the following statements. Check (√) whether each statement is True or False. If a statement is false, rewrite it so that it is true. Then go back to the passage and find the line that supports your answer.

1. ____ True ____ False Larry was blind when he was born.

____

2. ____ True ____ False Larry's doctors helped him when he was a young man.

____

3. ____ True ____ False Jenny found information to help her husband.

____

4. ____ True ____ False Doctors put a special device inside each of Larry's eyes.

____

5. ____ True ____ False The bionic eye helps Larry see again, but not as a normal person can see.

____

Reading Analysis

Read each question carefully. Circle the letter or the number of the correct answer.

1. Larry had a **serious eye disease**.
   a. **Serious** means
      1. unusual.
      2. very bad.
      3. new.
   b. His **eye disease**
      1. can make him blind.
      2. can easily improve.
      3. might make him wear glasses.

2. The part of Larry's eyes that sees light, the **retina**, was very weak.
   The **retina** can
   a. see different colors.
   b. see light and dark.
   c. see close and far away.

3. **Eventually**, Larry became blind.
   Eventually means
   a. slowly, over time.
   b. quickly, in a short time.
   c. unfortunately.

4. Jenny read a story about a new **device** that might help Larry.
   A **device** is
   a. a story or article.
   b. an instrument or tool.
   c. a doctor or surgeon.

5. Researchers developed a **bionic**, or robotic, eye.
   Bionic means
   a. an eye from another person.
   b. an eye made of electronic parts.
   c. an eye from an animal.

6. This device is a **replacement** for the retina. This device
   a. fixes the weak retina.
   b. takes the place of the weak retina.
   c. is better than the weak retina.

7. The retina is the part of the eye that **responds to** light.

   Responds to means

   a. reacts to.
   b. takes in.
   c. understands.

8. The Hesters met with Dr. Paul Hahn, an eye **surgeon** from the Duke Eye Center.

   A **surgeon**

   a. studies eye diseases.
   b. performs operations.
   c. studies blind people.

9. Dr. Hahn **placed** one of these devices in each of Larry's eyes.

   Placed means

   a. planned.
   b. attached.
   c. put.

10. Special glasses are **connected** to the device.

    Connected means

    a. controlled.
    b. surrounded.
    c. attached.

11. **At that moment**, Larry saw light for the first time in 30 years.

    At that moment means

    a. in a moment.
    b. immediately.
    c. slowly.

12. Larry was unable to **describe** his feelings, but he was very happy.

    Describe means

    a. talk about.
    b. be happy about.
    c. be excited about.

13. **The bionic eye picks up light signals from the camera.**

    a. A **signal** is
       1. a type of message.
       2. a kind of light.
       3. a photograph.

b. This sentence means

1. the bionic eye sends light signals to the camera.
2. the bionic eye moves like a camera.
3. the bionic eye gets light signals from the camera.

14. But even with the device, these people cannot see **objects** clearly.
Objects are

a. things you can see and touch.
b. light and dark.
c. different colors.

15. Being able to see light and shapes is **amazing** to people who could only see darkness.
Amazing means

a. new.
b. terrible.
c. wonderful.

16. What is the main idea of this passage?

a. For people who were born blind, a bionic eye can help them see for the first time.
b. For some people who became blind, a bionic eye can help them see light and shapes.
c. A bionic eye is a very good replacement for everyone.

Vocabulary Skills

PART 1

Recognizing Word Forms

In English, some adjectives become nouns by adding the suffix *-ness*, for example, *sad (adj.), sadness (n.).*

Complete each sentence with the correct word form on the left. The nouns are all singular.

bright *(adj.)*
brightness *(n.)*

1. Larry saw a ______________ light for the first time in over 30 years.
The ______________ was very exciting to him.

weak *(adj.)*
weakness *(n.)*

2. The retinas in both of Larry's eyes were very ______________. As the ______________ of his retinas became worse, Larry slowly became blind.

dark *(adj.)*
darkness *(n.)*

3. Larry's world was completely ______________ for 30 years. The ______________ disappeared when he received the new device.

blind *(adj.)*
blindness *(n.)*

4. Larry was ______________ for over 30 years. Now, with the bionic eye, Larry's complete ______________ is gone. He can see light and shapes.

happy *(adj.)*
happiness *(n.)*

5. Larry and his wife, Jenny, are very ______________. Their ______________ is even greater because Larry's life is so much better today.

PART 2

Understanding Antonyms

Antonyms are words with opposite meanings, for example, *hot* and *cold*.

Match each word with its antonym. Write the letter of the correct answer and the word in the space provided.

g. worse	1. better	a. complicated
______	2. easy	b. dark
______	3. light	c. difficult
______	4. serious	d. strong
______	5. simple	e. not bad
______	6. special	f. usual
______	7. weak	~~g. worse~~

Vocabulary in Context

Read the following sentences. Complete each sentence with the correct word from the box. Use each word only once.

amazing *(adj.)*	connected *(v.)*	eventually *(adv.)*	serious *(adj.)*
clearly *(adv.)*	device *(n.)*	replacement *(n.)*	weak *(adj.)*

1. I ______________ my laptop to the Internet a few hours ago. Now I can write and send email.
2. Olivia studied hard in her language classes. ______________, she learned to speak English very well.
3. Linda carried her little son's heavy backpack. He was too ______________ to carry it by himself.
4. I think I need new glasses. I can't see ______________ with these.
5. My new watch is ______________. I can use it to go online!
6. My car's GPS is a ______________ that helps me find directions quickly.
7. Jeff had a ______________ accident. He fell down the stairs and broke his leg.
8. Anna is buying a ______________ for her old backpack. Her old backpack is torn and the zipper is broken.

Reading Skill

Understanding a Graphic

Graphics often accompany a reading. They often illustrate information in the reading. Understanding this type of illustration increases your understanding of a reading.

Look at the graphic below. Match each statement to a number on the graphic.

How the Bionic Eye Works

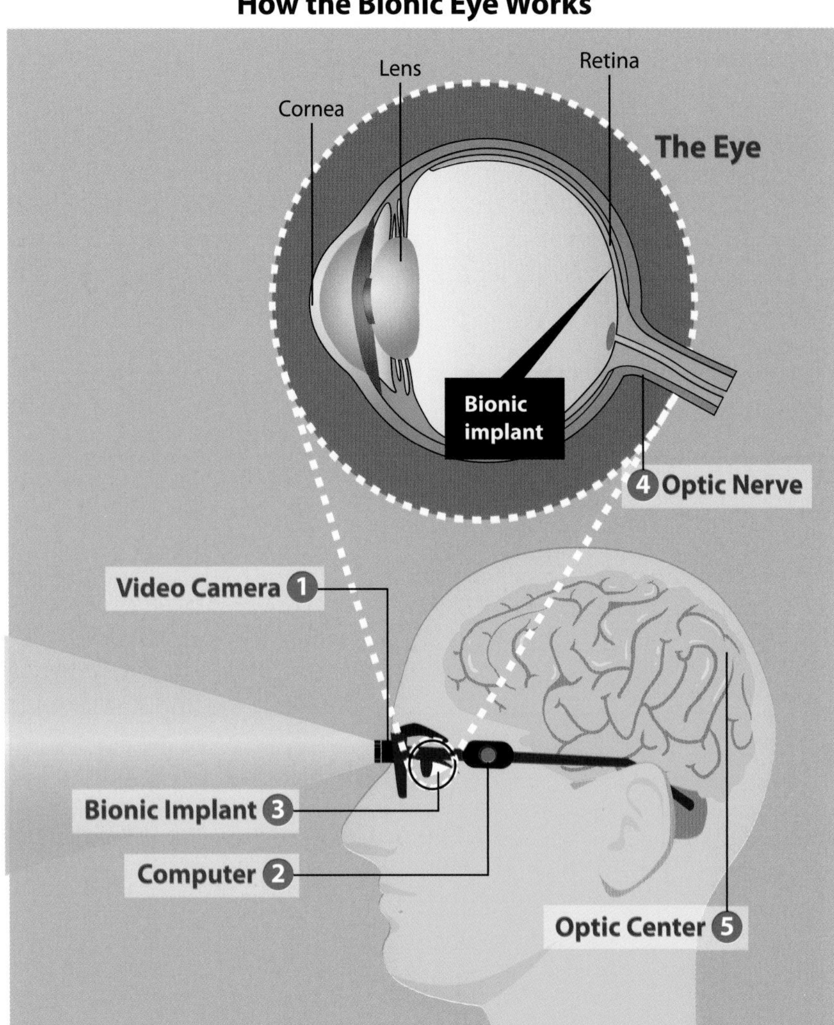

Source: http://photonics.com/Article,aspx?AID=35657

__2__ A computer changes the image into signals. The computer sends the signals to the bionic implant.

______ The optic center in the brain changes the signals into the images we see.

______ A video camera is attached to a pair of glasses. The video camera films an image.

______ The optic nerve carries the signals to the optic center in the brain.

______ The bionic implant is attached to the damaged retina. The implant uses the signals to stimulate the optic nerve.

Amanda Kitts ties a student's shoelaces.

Another Look

CD 2 TR 4 **Read the following passage about a teacher with a bionic arm. Then answer the questions that follow.**

A Bionic Hug

Amanda Kitts is the owner of three day care centers in Knoxville, Tennessee. She loves to take care of the children, dry their tears, and hug them. She also loves to hug her son, Casey. "These kids are my life," she said. "They fill my heart with love." However, Amanda had a terrible car accident several years ago. She was hurt very badly in the accident. Amanda lost her left arm as a result of the accident. "It hurt me to think that I may never be able to hug Casey and the children again," she said.

Amanda's husband searched the Internet for information to help Amanda. One day, he found some news about the Rehabilitation Institute of Chicago. There, doctors developed a new kind of artificial limb. He believed it could help his wife. This artificial arm uses Amanda's nerve signals in her brain to control it. "I don't really think about it. I just move it," says Amanda. "I'm just excited all the time because they keep improving the arm. One day, I'll be able to feel things with it and clap my hands together to the songs my kids are singing."

Amanda is not the only person who is excited. The children at the day care centers are excited, too. "Hey kids! How are my babies today?" she asks. "The robot arm!" several children say happily. "Make it do something silly!" one girl says. "Silly? Remember how I can shake your hand?" Amanda asks. A boy reaches out and shakes her hand. But it wasn't always easy for Amanda to do this.

Amanda had to learn how to use her new arm. "It was difficult at first," she says. "I would try to move it, and it wouldn't always go where I wanted." However, she worked hard. Slowly, she was able to use it more and more. "It was wonderful," she says. "My new arm made me feel like I could do anything again." Most importantly to Amanda, her new arm is perfect for hugging!

QUESTIONS FOR ANOTHER LOOK

1. How does Amanda Kitts feel about the children in her day care centers? What does Amanda especially like to do with them and her son, too?

2. What happened to Amanda?

3. What does Amanda have now? What can she do with it?

4. How do the children feel about Amanda's artificial arm?

Topics for Discussion and Writing

1. What are some other kinds of medical technology that help people? How do these kinds of technology help?

2. Is technology important in your everyday life? Why or why not? Explain your answer.

4. Write in your journal. Larry Hester and Amanda Kitts had big changes in their lives. Write about a big change in your life. When did it occur? What happened?

Critical Thinking

1. Medical technology improves every day. Go online. What are some new kinds of medical technology? Who can the new technology help?

2. Work with a partner. Make a list of the technology you use every day. How does it help you? Compare your list with your classmates' lists and make a class list.

3. Medical technology helped Larry Hester, who was blind, and Amanda Kitts, who lost her arm in an accident. Medical technology helps many other people with disabilities. Go online. Find someone with a different disability. How did medical technology help him or her?

4. Larry used his memory to help him get around at home and at work. How did his memory help him? Discuss this with a partner.

5. Larry and others with bionic eyes can only see light and shapes. Do you think these bionic eyes are really helpful to blind people, or are they a waste of time? Discuss your ideas with your classmates.

Amanda Kitts and her bionic arm

Crossword Puzzle

Review the words in the box. Then read the clues on the next page. Write the words in the correct spaces in the puzzle.

amazing	darkness	eventually	retina
bionic	describe	light	serious
blind	device	replacement	signal
connect	disease	respond	technology

Crossword Puzzle Clues

ACROSS CLUES

3. There is a part of the eye that can __________, or react, to light.

5. There are several __________ conditions that can cause people to lose their sight.

6. A camera sends an electronic __________ to the robotic eye.

7. A __________ person is unable to see.

9. Could you __________ the apartment to me? How many rooms does it have?

10. __________ is improving every day. One day, Larry may be able to see normally.

13. The robotic eye is a __________ for a specific part of the eye.

14. The robotic eye allows Larry to see __________ and shapes.

15. A __________ eye is made up of electronic parts.

DOWN CLUES

1. Before Larry had his eye surgery, he lived in a world of __________.

2. You need to __________, or attach, a special pair of glasses to a camera.

4. __________, researchers may be able to develop a robotic eye that will allow people to see normally.

8. Larry had an eye __________ that caused him to lose his sight.

9. A robotic eye is a special __________ that enables people to see light and shapes.

11. Wonderful

12. The __________ is the part of the eye that reacts to light.

UNIT 5

International Scientists

Scientist Neil deGrasse Tyson visits an old laboratory.

1. Who are some famous scientists? Why are they famous?
2. What do people win a Nobel Prize for?

CHAPTER 9 Alfred Nobel: A Man of Peace

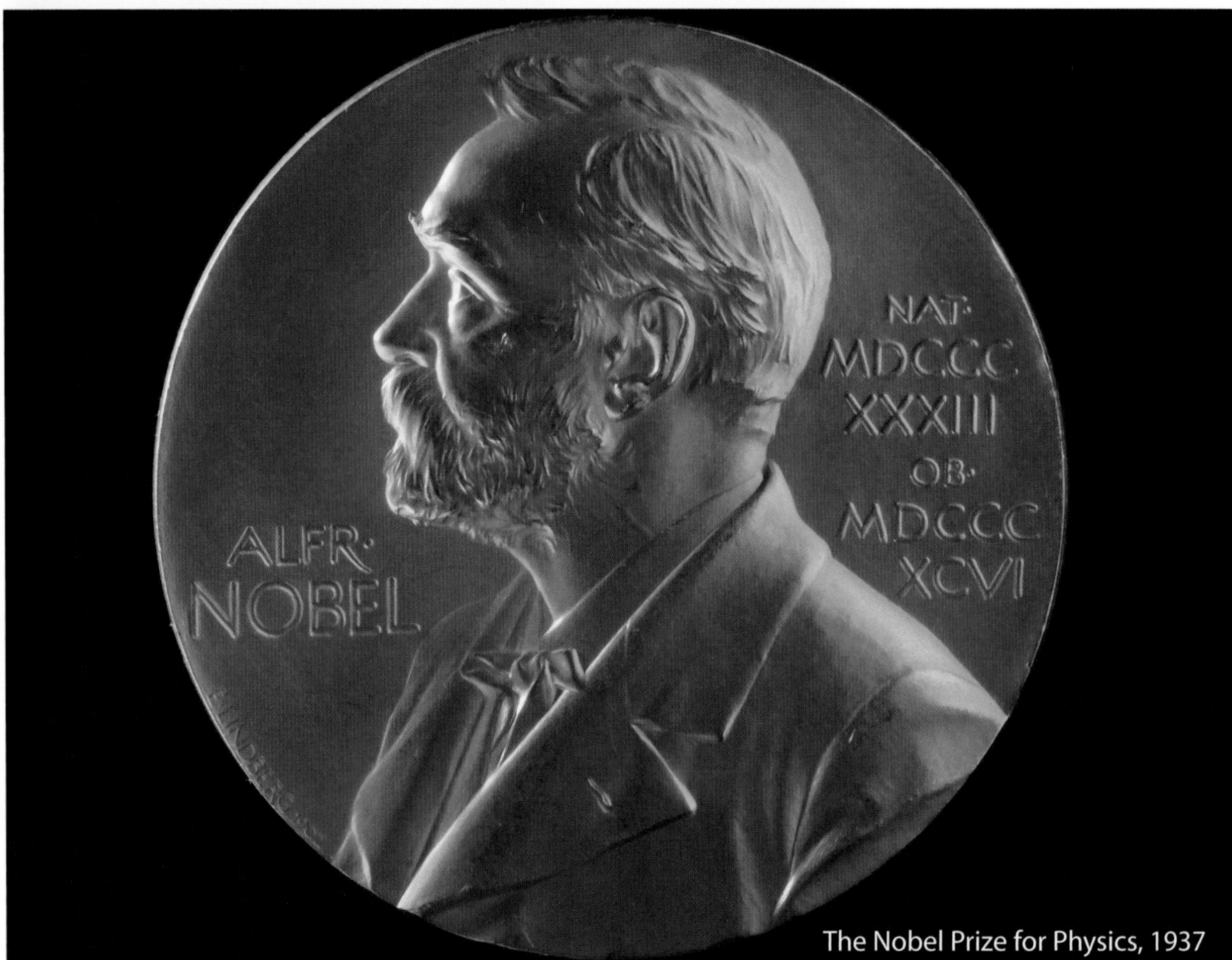

The Nobel Prize for Physics, 1937

Prereading

Discuss these questions with a partner.

1. Look at the photo. This medal is a Nobel Prize. Alfred Nobel's image is in the center of the medal. Why is Alfred Nobel famous?

a. He established the Nobel Prize.
b. He lived in the 19th century.
c. He invented dynamite.
d. He was Swedish.

2. What do you know about Alfred Nobel? Work with a partner. Make a list.

____

____

____

3. Read the title of this chapter. Why do you think Alfred Nobel is called a man of peace?

____

____

Reading

Read the following passage carefully. Then complete the exercises that follow.

Alfred Nobel: A Man of Peace

The headline in the newspaper announced the death of Alfred Nobel on April 13, 1888. The reporter called him a salesman of death, "The Dynamite King," because he invented this powerful explosive. In fact, Alfred Nobel's dynamite business made him a very rich man. The newspaper story continued, giving Alfred Nobel's age, nationality, and other information about his business. However, the words "The Dynamite King" were all that the 55-year-old Swedish man read.

Alfred Nobel unhappily put down the newspaper. No, he wasn't dead—his brother Ludwig died the day before, and the French newspaper made a mistake. All the same, Alfred Nobel was disturbed. Was this the way the world was going to remember him? He thought this was unfair. He spent his life working for peace in the world. He hated violence and war. He invented dynamite to save lives. He wanted people to remember him as a man of peace.

In the 19th century, people used nitroglycerin, an explosive substance, but it was very unsafe. At that time, many countries were beginning to build railroads and tunnels. They needed a safe, powerful explosive to construct railroad tracks through mountains. People also needed dynamite to blow up stone in order to construct buildings, dams, and roads. Alfred Nobel invented dynamite for these peaceful uses. Moreover, he believed that if all countries had the same powerful weapons, wars would end. In fact, this was a popular idea of his day.

Nobel was very upset about the image that the world had of him, but he did not know what to do about it. He thought about his problem for years. He wanted to think of the best way for people to use his fortune of $9 million after his death. Then in 1895, an adventurer named Salomon August Andrée made plans for an expedition to reach the North Pole. People all over the world were excited about Andrée's journey. Nobel read about Andrée's plan, too, and had an inspiration. He finally knew what to do with his fortune. He wrote his Last Will and Testament.[1] In his will, he instructed people to use all of his money for an annual, or yearly, award as an honor to leaders of science, literature, and world peace. He stated that these leaders could be men or women of any nationality.

Alfred Nobel died on December 10, 1896, at the age of 63. He was unmarried and had no children. People all over the world wondered who was going to get Nobel's money. They were amazed when they learned of Nobel's plan to award annual prizes in the fields of physics, chemistry, medicine, literature, and peace. They awarded the first Nobel Prizes in 1901. The Nobel Prize very soon became the greatest honor that a person could receive in these fields. In 1969, they added an award for economics.

The report of Alfred Nobel's death was a mistake, but the decision that he made because of this error gave the world the image of him that he wanted. Nobel established the Nobel Prize, and the world thinks of him the way he wanted to be remembered: Alfred Nobel, man of peace.

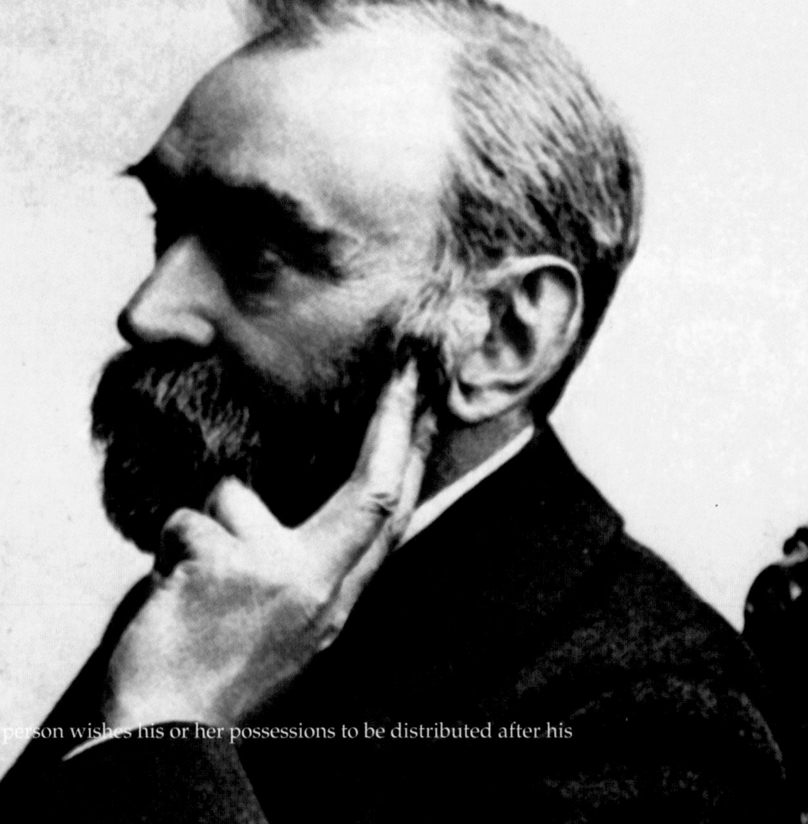

Chemist and inventor Alfred Nobel

[1] **Last Will and Testament:** A legal paper that states how a person wishes his or her possessions to be distributed after his or her death.

Fact Finding

Read the passage again. Then read the following statements. Check (√) whether each statement is True or False. If a statement is false, rewrite it so that it is true. Then go back to the passage and find the line that supports your answer.

1. _____ True _____ False Alfred Nobel wanted people to remember him as "The Dynamite King."

____

2. _____ True _____ False Alfred Nobel died in 1888.

____

3. _____ True _____ False Alfred Nobel invented dynamite.

____

4. _____ True _____ False Alfred Nobel hated violence.

____

5. _____ True _____ False Only men can receive a Nobel Prize.

____

6. _____ True _____ False In 1895, Salomon August Andrée received the first Nobel Prize.

____

Reading Analysis

Read each question carefully. Circle the letter or the number of the correct answer, or write your answer in the space provided.

1. The **headline** in the newspaper announced the death of Alfred Nobel on April 13, 1888.
A **headline** is

a. a line at the top of the newspaper with the day's date.
b. a line in the newspaper with the writer's name on it.
c. the title at the top of a newspaper story.

2. The newspaper story continued, giving Alfred Nobel's age, nationality, and other information about his business. **However**, the words "The Dynamite King" were all that the 55-year-old Swedish man read.

a. **However** means

1. and.
2. but.
3. then.

b. Complete the second sentence with the correct choice.

Robert wanted to go to the beach. However,

1. it rained, so he stayed home.
2. he asked his friends to go with him.
3. he brought his lunch and a big umbrella.

c. **However, the words "The Dynamite King" were all that the 55-year-old Swedish man read.**

What does this sentence mean?

1. He read everything in the newspaper story.
2. These three words were the only words he really looked at.
3. He did not read the whole newspaper.

3. Nobel invented dynamite, a powerful **explosive**.

An **explosive** is

a. something that can blow up.
b. a new invention.
c. an award.

4. **Ludwig died the day before, and the French newspaper made a mistake. All the same, Alfred Nobel was disturbed.**

a. **Disturbed** means

1. unsure.
2. happy.
3. upset.

b. What do these sentences mean?

1. Because the news was a mistake, Alfred was not upset anymore.
2. It did not matter that the news was a mistake. Alfred was still upset.
3. Alfred was upset that the news about his brother was unfair.

5. Read line 10: He thought this was **unfair**.

a. **Unfair** means

1. new.
2. good.
3. wrong.

b. Nobel thought it was unfair that
   1. the newspaper said his brother died.
   2. the newspaper called him "a salesman of death."
   3. the newspaper made a mistake.

6. He hated **violence** and war.

Violence means
   a. mistakes or errors.
   b. bad ideas.
   c. harm or damage.

7. Nobel invented dynamite to **save lives**.

Save lives means
   a. help people live.
   b. help people work.
   c. help people hurt other people.

8. People needed a safe, powerful explosive to **construct** railroad tracks through mountains.

Construct means
   a. build.
   b. blow up.
   c. plan.

9. Alfred Nobel invented dynamite for these peaceful uses. **Moreover**, he believed that if all countries had the same powerful weapons, wars would end. This was a popular idea of **his day**.

   a. **Moreover** means
      1. however.
      2. in addition.
      3. as a result.
   b. Complete the second sentence with the correct choice.
   Sara needed to learn English because she wanted to go to college in the United States. Moreover,
      1. she had to speak English to get a good job.
      2. she hated to study and was a poor student.
   c. **His day** refers to
      1. the day Nobel invented dynamite.
      2. the year 1895.
      3. the time that he lived.

10. Nobel was very upset about the **image** that the world had of him.

Image means
   a. announcement.
   b. idea or thought.
   c. photograph.

11. Nobel wanted to think of the best way for people to use his **fortune** of $9 million after his death.

What is a synonym of **fortune**?

a. Idea
b. Plan
c. Wealth

12. In 1895, an adventurer named Salomon August Andrée made plans for an **expedition** to reach the North Pole.

An **expedition** is

a. a special journey made by a group of people.
b. a trip to a faraway location.
c. an exciting trip to a foreign country.

13. In 1895, Alfred Nobel wrote his **Last Will and Testament**. In his will, he instructed people to use all of his money for an **annual**, or yearly, award.

a. Look at page 140. What is a **Last Will and Testament**?

____

____

b. Where did you find this information?

____

c. This information is called a
   1. direction.
   2. footnote.
   3. preface.

d. An **annual** award is given out
   1. once a year.
   2. five times a year.
   3. six times a year.

14. People were **amazed** when they learned of Nobel's plan to award annual prizes in the **fields** of physics, chemistry, medicine, literature, and peace.

a. **Amazed** means
   1. angry.
   2. surprised.
   3. happy.

b. **Field** means
   1. an occupation.
   2. a subject; area.
   3. an outdoor area.

15. The report of Alfred Nobel's death was a **mistake**, but the decision that he made because of this error gave the world the image that he wanted.
In this sentence, which word is a synonym of **mistake**?

____

16. What is the main idea of this reading?

a. Alfred Nobel wrote his will after Andrée went to the North Pole.
b. The Nobel Prize is an internationally famous award.
c. Alfred Nobel was a peaceful man who gave the world a great prize.

Vocabulary Skills

PART 1

Recognizing Word Forms

In English, some verbs become nouns by adding the suffix *-ion* or *-ation,* for example, *suggest (v.), suggestion (n.).* Some words change spelling, for example, *combine (v.), combination (n.).*

Complete each sentence with the correct word form on the left. Write all the verbs in the simple past. The nouns may be singular or plural.

instruct *(v.)*	**1.** Alfred Nobel ______________ people to use his money for a yearly
instruction *(n.)*	award. The people followed these ______________ very carefully.
invent *(v.)*	**2.** Alfred Nobel's ______________ saved the lives of many people.
invention *(n.)*	He ______________ a useful explosive.
construct *(v.)*	**3.** In the 19th century, many countries ______________ bridges and
construction *(n.)*	tunnels. This kind of ______________ can be very dangerous.

inspire ***(v.)*** **4.** Salomon August Andrée ________________ Alfred Nobel to use his

inspiration ***(n.)*** fortune to honor leaders of the world. The Nobel Prize started because of this ________________.

continue ***(v.)*** **5.** People ________________ to remember Alfred Nobel as a peaceful man

continuation ***(n.)*** after his death. The ________________ of this image was important to Nobel.

PART 2

Understanding the Prefix *un-*

In English, the prefix *un-* means *not*, for example, *unmarried* means *not married,* and *unfinished* means *not finished.*

Read the following sentences. Complete each sentence with the correct word from the box.

unfair	unhappily	unpopular	unsafe	unusual

1. Alfred Nobel ________________ put down his newspaper after he read the headline.
2. The reporter called Nobel a salesman of death. Nobel thought this idea was ________________.
3. Alfred Nobel's Last Will and Testament was very ________________. He gave all his money for the Nobel Prize.
4. Nitroglycerin was a very ________________ explosive. It hurt many people.
5. Alfred Nobel was very ________________ because he invented dynamite.

Vocabulary in Context

Read the following sentences. Complete each sentence with the correct word or phrase from the box. Use each word or phrase only once.

all the same	award *(n.)*	field *(n.)*	mistake *(n.)*
amaze *(v.)*	disturb *(v.)*	fortune *(n.)*	moreover

1. Chris works in the ______________________ of medicine. He is a nurse.
2. Carolyn moved to the city to be close to the university. ______________________, her family lives in the city, so she can visit them more often now.
3. Jason didn't have any children, so he left his ______________________ to his nephews after he died.
4. Magicians always ______________________ people with their tricks. They can pull rabbits out of their hats!
5. I made a ______________________ on my test. I wrote, "two" instead of "too."
6. Please don't ______________________ Serena when she is studying. She needs to concentrate on her homework.
7. The students were very tired after class. ______________________, they did their homework and studied hard when they came home.
8. The university gave Nicole a special ______________________ because of her excellent work.

Reading Skill

Creating a Chart to Summarize a Reading

It is important to be able to create charts. They help you organize information and understand it better.

Read the passage again. Write the information in the chart below.

Alfred Nobel		
Accomplishment	**Reason**	**Result**
1. *He invented dynamite.*		
2.		

Another Look

CD 2 TR 6 **Read the following passage about how Nobel Prize winners are chosen. Then answer the questions that follow.**

Choosing Nobel Prize Winners

Alfred Nobel gave more than $9 million of his fortune to establish annual Nobel Prizes. According to Nobel's instructions, the Nobel Foundation gives money to people who help humankind in some outstanding way in these five fields: physics, chemistry, physiology (or medicine), literature, and peace. In addition to the cash prize, each Nobel Prize winner receives a gold medal.

The Nobel Foundation is the legal owner of the prize funds, but it does not award the prizes. The foundation follows a list of Alfred Nobel's rules. One of the rules states that the foundation does not have to give out all of the prizes each year. In fact, it did not give out Nobel Prizes for the years 1940–1942.

Different groups give out each award. The Royal Swedish Academy of Sciences gives the physics and chemistry awards. The Karolinska Institute of Stockholm, Sweden, awards the physiology or medicine prize. The Swedish Academy awards the Nobel Prize in Literature. The Norwegian parliament chooses a committee of five people to award the Nobel Peace Prize. In 1969, the committee established a sixth prize in economics. The Royal Swedish Academy of Sciences gives this award, too.

Each of these institutions must receive the names of candidates before February 1 of each year. A jury of 12 people decides on a final candidate by majority vote. If there is no majority vote for any one candidate, the prize is not offered that year. The jury reviews the candidates and asks them many questions, including the following:

- Did you make the outstanding contribution in the previous year?
- Was your contribution the result of many years of research?
- Did you work with one, two, or three scientists as a team? (The prize may be divided.)
- Did your discovery depend on the work of another candidate? (Again, the prize may be divided.)

Committees awarded the first Nobel Prizes on December 10, 1901, the fifth anniversary of Alfred Nobel's death. The amount of each prize was more than $40,000 at that time. Today each prize is more than $1.4 million.

Liberian peace activist Leymah Gbowee receives the 2011 Nobel Peace Prize.

QUESTIONS FOR ANOTHER LOOK

1. _____ True _____ False The Nobel Foundation must give out each award every year.
2. Why do you think no prizes were given out from 1940 to 1942?

   ____

3. What happens if the jury of 12 people cannot agree on one candidate?

   ____

4. Read the interview question again: "Did you make the outstanding contribution in the previous year?" Why do you think this information is important?

   ____

   ____

Topics for Discussion and Writing

1. Pretend that you are wealthy. What do you want to happen to your property and money after you die? Write instructions.
2. Nominate a famous person for a Nobel Prize in one of the six fields. Describe the person. Why does he or she deserve the Nobel Prize? Explain your reasons.
3. Go online and find the list of all of the Nobel Prize winners. Select one of the Nobel Prize winners. Write about him or her and tell why you think this person deserved the award.
4. Write a short biography of one of the Nobel Prize winners who interests you.
5. Write in your journal. Describe how you want people to remember you. Explain why you want people to remember you in this way.

Critical Thinking

1. Work in a group of three or four. You are part of a committee that has to decide on a new category for the Nobel Prize. Remember, the fields now are physics, chemistry, medicine/physiology, literature, peace, and economics. Why do you think this seventh prize is a good idea? Discuss your reasons. Compare your ideas with those of your classmates. Then take a class vote to decide on the new category.

2. Work in a group of three or four. You are part of a committee that has to decide to eliminate one category from the Nobel Prize awards. Discuss the reasons you think this prize is no longer necessary or desirable. Compare your reasons with those of your classmates. Take a vote to decide on which category to eliminate.

3. Go online. Search for a website that lists all of the Nobel Prize winners. Make a list of the Nobel Prize winners from your country and/or another country you are interested in. Write down the year that each person on your list received the prize and his or her field. Then choose one person, and write about his or her achievement.

4. Alfred Nobel invented dynamite to help people build railroads, tunnels, buildings, and dams, but the reporter in the story called Nobel "a salesman of death." Why? Discuss your ideas with your classmates.

5. Nobel established the Nobel Prize so that people would remember him as a man of peace. What other reasons do you think he had for wanting to give prizes to people who were leaders in their fields? Discuss your ideas with a partner.

Crossword Puzzle

Review the words in the box. Then read the clues on the next page. Write the words in the correct spaces in the puzzle.

amazed	dynamite	fortune	moreover
award	expedition	headline	peace
construct	explosive	image	violence
disturbed	field	mistake	will

Crossword Puzzle Clues

ACROSS CLUES

4. To build a railroad, you need people, material, and a plan. __________, you need a lot of money.

7. Nobel hated fighting and war. He hated all kinds of __________.

12. Nine million dollars is a lot of money. To many people it is a __________.

13. __________ is the invention that made Alfred Nobel rich.

15. The Nobel Prize is an __________ for a person's achievements.

16. Error

DOWN CLUES

1. Surprised

2. The opposite of war

3. A __________ states how a person wishes his or her possessions to be distributed after death.

5. The scientists are planning an __________ to the mountains of South America.

6. Chemistry is a __________ of study.

8. Bombs are __________. They blow up when they hit something.

9. Upset

10. The company plans to __________ a new bridge across the river.

11. A __________ is the title of a newspaper article.

14. Today, people have the __________ of Nobel that he really wanted: as a man of peace.

CHAPTER 10 Marie Curie: Nobel Prize Winner

Marie Curie in her laboratory

Prereading

Work with a partner to discuss these questions.

1. Look at the photo of Marie Curie, who was a Nobel Prize winner.

a. What was Marie Curie's profession?
   1. She was a doctor.
   2. She was a scientist.
   3. She was an inventor.

b. What kind of work did Marie Curie do?
   1. She helped sick people.
   2. She invented new chemicals.
   3. She did research.

c. Where did Marie Curie do most of her work?
   1. In a laboratory
   2. In a hospital
   3. In an office

2. Read the title of this chapter. What do you think Marie Curie won the Nobel Prize for?

a. Economics
b. Physics
c. Chemistry
d. Medicine
e. Peace
f. Literature

3. How many times do you think Marie Curie won a Nobel Prize?

a. Once
b. Twice
c. Three times

Reading

CD 2 TR 7

Read the following passage carefully. Then complete the exercises that follow.

Marie Curie: Nobel Prize Winner

Maria Sklodowska was born on November 7, 1867, in Poland. Maria's father wanted his five children to become well educated. Unfortunately, the family was poor. In fact, Maria worked for six years to support her older sister Bronya so Bronya could study medicine at the Sorbonne in Paris. When Bronya finished medical school in 1891, 23-year-old Maria Sklodowska went to Paris to begin her own education.

Once she arrived in Paris, Maria changed her name to the French form, Marie. After living with Bronya and her husband for a short time, she moved to an inexpensive apartment near the university so she could study without interruption. When Marie was a student, she was extremely poor. However, in spite of her difficult living conditions, she was happy.

In July 1893, Marie passed her physics examination. She was first in her class. At this time, she met Pierre Curie, a young scientist. Marie and Pierre discovered that they had a lot in common. They both believed that science was the most important part of their lives. They didn't care about money or about being comfortable. They fell in love and got married on July 26, 1895. Marie and Pierre Curie were very happy. They discussed their work and the latest scientific events, such as the discovery of X-rays.[1] Marie was interested in this research and began to look for unknown

[1] **X-rays:** An invisible, high-energy form of light that can pass through many solid objects such as the human body.

elements that had such rays. Pierre Curie stopped his own research in order to assist Marie with her work. He realized that she was about to make an important discovery.

In 1898, the Curies discovered two new elements that gave off radiation. They named these elements polonium and radium. In those days, no one knew that such radioactive materials were dangerous. In fact, Marie Curie created the word "radioactive" to describe these materials. They did not know that exposure to this radioactivity caused their constant fatigue and illnesses, so they kept working. Finally, in 1902, they proved the existence of radium.

On June 25, 1903, Marie became the first woman to receive a doctor of science degree from the Sorbonne. Then she received an even greater award. In 1903, the Academy of Science in Stockholm, Sweden, awarded the Nobel Prize in Physics to Marie and Pierre Curie and Henri Becquerel for their discoveries in radioactivity. The Curies continued to work closely together until a tragic event occurred. On a rainy day in April 1906, Pierre was killed in a street accident. Marie was heartbroken, but she continued working. Then, in 1910, she isolated radium. It was the biggest accomplishment of Marie Curie's career. In 1911, she received the Nobel Prize again, this time for her work in the field of chemistry. She was the first woman to receive the Nobel Prize and the first person to receive it a second time.

Over the years, Marie's constant exposure to radiation continued to destroy her health. She died on July 4, 1934, from an illness caused by her life's work: radium. Marie Curie never cared about making any money from her discoveries. Her life had been one of hard work, perseverance, and self-sacrifice. However, in her personal life, she was happily married and had two daughters. Professionally, she made important discoveries and achieved greatness in her field.

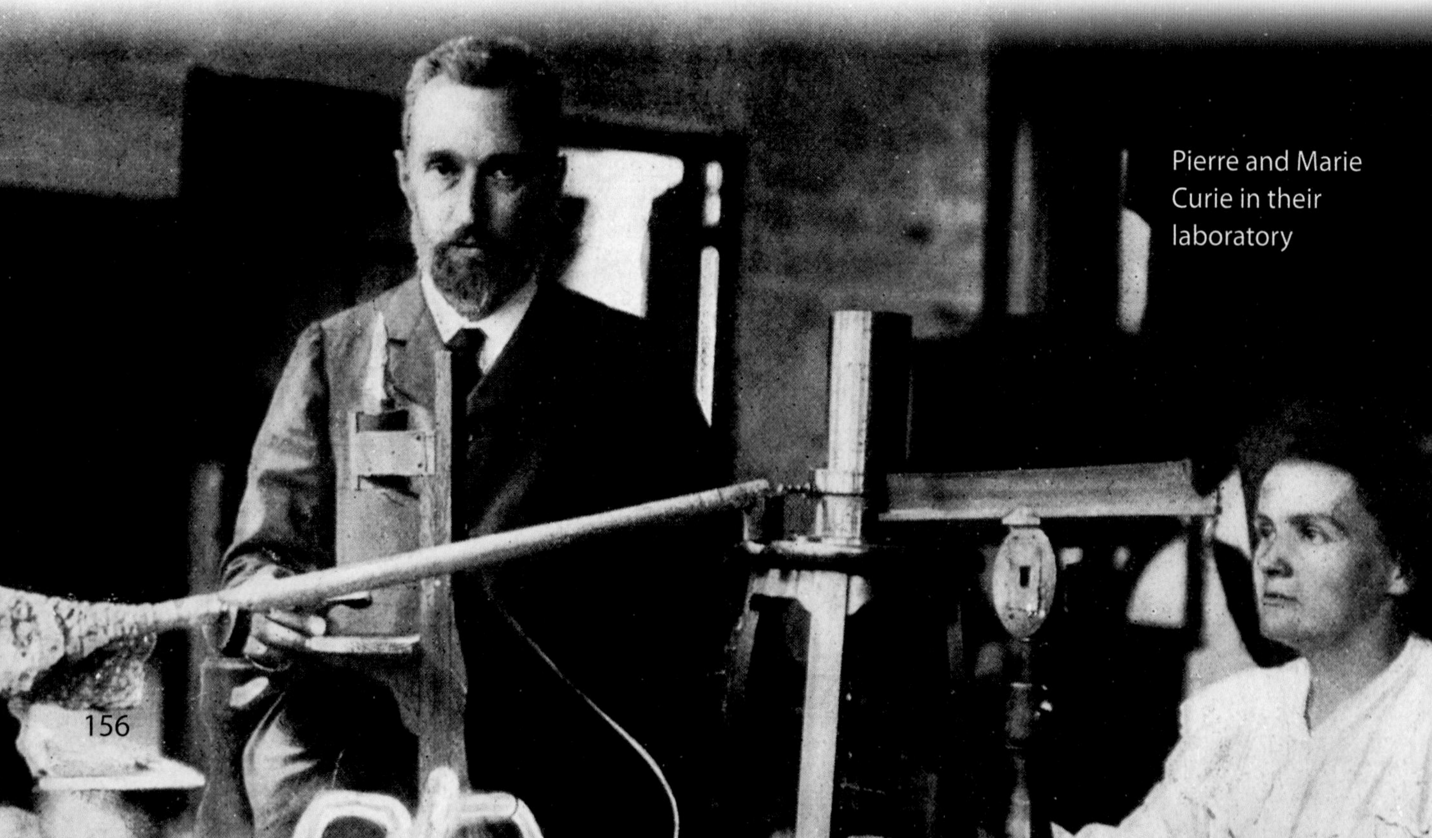

Pierre and Marie Curie in their laboratory

Fact Finding

Read the passage again. Then read the following statements. Check (√) whether each statement is True or False. If a statement is false, rewrite it so that it is true. Then go back to the passage and find the line that supports your answer.

1. _____ True _____ False Marie Curie was Maria Sklodowska.

____

2. _____ True _____ False Marie Curie was born in Paris.

____

3. _____ True _____ False Marie went to the University of Poland.

____

4. _____ True _____ False Marie's husband, Pierre, was a scientist.

____

5. _____ True _____ False The Curies discovered two new elements.

____

6. _____ True _____ False Radium made the Curies feel tired and sick.

____

7. _____ True _____ False Marie Curie was the first person to receive the Nobel Prize.

____

8. _____ True _____ False Marie Curie won the Nobel Prize twice.

____

9. _____ True _____ False Marie Curie wanted to earn a lot of money.

____

Reading Analysis

Read each question carefully. Circle the letter or the number of the correct answer, or write your answer in the space provided.

1. Maria's father wanted his five children to become well educated.
Unfortunately, the family was poor.

a. How many brothers and sisters did Maria have?

b. This sentence means that
   1. none of the children went to a university.
   2. all the children went to a university.
   3. the family could not afford to send the children to a university.

c. Complete the second sentence with the correct choice.
   Marie and Pierre Curie worked well together for many years.
   Unfortunately,
   1. Pierre died when he was still young.
   2. Pierre and Marie discovered two new elements.
   3. Pierre and Marie shared the Nobel Prize in 1903.

2. The family was poor. **In fact**, Maria supported her older sister Bronya until she finished medical school at the **Sorbonne** in Paris.

a. The second sentence means that
   1. Maria lived with her sister.
   2. Maria gave her sister money to live on.
   3. Maria helped her sister study.

b. What information follows **in fact**?
   1. Additional information that gives more details about the previous sentence
   2. Different information that introduces a new idea

c. The **Sorbonne** is
   1. a business.
   2. a hospital.
   3. a school.

3. **Once** she arrived in Paris, Maria changed her name to the French form, Marie.
In this context, **once** means

a. one time.
b. when.
c. before.

4. Marie moved to an inexpensive apartment near the university so she could study **without interruption**.

Without interruption means

1. without anyone stopping her.
2. without having to travel.
3. without having to pay a lot of money.

5. When Marie was a student, she was extremely poor. However, **in spite of** her **difficult living conditions**, she was happy.

a. The second sentence means that

1. Marie's living conditions made her happy because they were difficult.
2. Marie's living conditions were bad, but she was happy.

b. Read the following sentences. Write **in spite of** in the appropriate sentence.

1. John was very sick. ____________ his illness, he went to work.
2. John was very sick. ____________ his illness, he went to the hospital.

c. **Difficult living conditions** refers to the fact that

1. Marie lived in a cold, uncomfortable apartment and ate little food.
2. Marie was a student and had to study hard.

6. In July 1893, Marie passed her physics exam. She was **first in her class**. **At this time**, she met Pierre Curie, a young scientist.

a. What does **first in her class** mean?

1. Marie graduated before all the other students.
2. Marie was the best student in her class.

b. **At this time** means

1. at the same time she passed her exam.
2. in the 1890s.
3. during this time period.

7. Marie and Pierre Curie discussed their work and the latest scientific **events**, such as the discovery of **X-rays**.

a. An **event** is

1. a type of work.
2. an important happening.
3. a special discovery.

b. What are **X-rays**?

____

____

c. Where did you look for this information?

____

____

d. This kind of information is called
   1. an instruction.
   2. an index.
   3. a footnote.

8. Pierre Curie stopped his own research **in order to assist** Marie.

a. Pierre Curie stopped his own research
   1. because he wanted to help Marie.
   2. because he wanted to tell Marie what to do.

b. What follows **in order to**?
   1. An example
   2. A result
   3. A reason

c. **Assist** means
   1. help.
   2. study.
   3. stop.

9. Pierre realized that Marie was **about to** make an important discovery.

About to means

a. the time immediately before something happens.
b. the time immediately after something happens.
c. at the moment something is happening.

10. In 1898, the Curies discovered two new **elements** that give off radiation. They named these elements polonium and radium. In those days, no one knew that such **radioactive** materials were dangerous.

a. A synonym for **elements** in this sentence is

   ______________________.

b. **Radioactive** elements are
   1. new.
   2. unknown.
   3. unsafe.

11. Marie Curie **created the term "radioactivity"** to describe these materials. The Curies did not know that **exposure** to radioactivity caused their illnesses.

a. **Created the term "radioactivity"** means that
   1. Marie Curie was the first person to use the word "radioactivity."
   2. Marie Curie invented these radioactive materials.

b. **Exposure** means
   1. working with something.
   2. being unprotected from something.
   3. creating something.

12. The Curies continued to work closely together **until** a **tragic** event occurred. On a rainy day in April 1906, Pierre was killed in a street accident. Marie was **heartbroken**, but she continued working.

a. **Until** means
   1. up to the time when something else happens.
   2. up to the time when something else finishes.

b. Read the following sentences. Write the word **until** in the appropriate sentence.
   1. John studied very hard ____________________ he finished the exam.
   2. John studied very hard ____________________ the exam began.

c. The word **tragic** means
   1. very violent.
   2. very sad.
   3. very surprising.

d. **Heartbroken** means that
   1. Marie was very unhappy.
   2. Marie became very sick.

13. **Over the years**, Marie's **constant** exposure to radiation continued to destroy her health.

a. **Over the years** means
   1. in the years immediately before Marie died.
   2. through all the years that she worked.

b. **Constant** means
   1. dangerous.
   2. radioactive.
   3. continuous.

14. Her life had been one of hard work, **perseverance**, and self-sacrifice. However, in her personal life, she was happily married and had two daughters. Professionally, she made important discoveries and achieved greatness in her **field**.

a. Think about Marie Curie's life. What does the characteristic of **perseverance** mean?
   1. Marie Curie had a sad life.
   2. Marie Curie never stopped trying.
   3. Marie Curie had little money.

b. What was Marie Curie's **field**?
   1. Paris
   2. Career
   3. Science

15. What is the main idea of this reading?

a. Marie Curie discovered two new elements: polonium and radium.
b. Marie Curie was a great scientist who won the Nobel Prize twice.
c. Marie Curie did research on radioactive materials for many years.

Vocabulary Skills

PART 1

Recognizing Word Forms

In English, some verbs become nouns by adding the suffixes *-ance* or *-ence,* for example, *persist (v.), persistence (n.).*

Complete each sentence with the correct word form on the left. Write all the verbs in the past. The nouns are all singular.

occur *(v.)*	**1.** The Curies worked together until a tragic event ________________, and
occurrence *(n.)*	Pierre died. His death was a tragic ________________.
exist *(v.)*	**2.** After years of hard work, Marie and Pierre Curie proved the ____________
existence *(n.)*	of radium. No one knew that radium ____________ until they discovered it.
persevere *(v.)*	**3.** Marie was having a lot of trouble with her work. However, she ____________.
perseverance *(n.)*	She became very successful because of her ________________.
assist *(v.)*	**4.** Pierre's ________________ was very helpful to his wife. He stopped his
assistance *(n.)*	work and ________________ Marie.
avoid *(v.)*	**5.** The Curies were very hard workers. They ________________ most things
avoidance *(n.)*	in their life except work. The ________________ of a comfortable life
	was necessary to their work.

PART 2

Understanding Synonyms

Synonyms are words that have the same or similar meanings, for example, *big* and *large*.

Match each word with its synonym. Write the letter of the correct answer and the word or phrase on the line provided.

c. achievement	1. accomplishment	a. cheap
________	2. constant	b. stop for a short time
________	3. element	~~c. achievement~~
________	4. extremely	d. continuous
________	5. illness	e. help financially
________	6. inexpensive	f. heartbreaking
________	7. interrupt	g. material
________	8. support	h. sickness
________	9. tragic	i. unhappily
________	10. unfortunately	j. very

Vocabulary in Context

Read the following sentences. Complete each sentence with the correct word or phrase from the box. Use each word or phrase only once.

elements *(n.)*	in spite of	once	perseverance *(n.)*
exposure *(n.)*	interruptions *(n.)*	over the years	tragic *(adj.)*

1. ________________ the rainy weather, Jane decided to take a walk in the park.

2. Thomas is well known for his ________________. He works hard and never stops trying.

3. It's hard for me to study at home because of the constant ________________. I prefer to study in the library, where it's always quiet.

4. We didn't know anyone when we moved here, but ________________ we've made a lot of friends.

5. ______________________ you complete the application form, you can take the entrance exam.

6. The fire in John's home was a ______________________ accident. He and his wife were very badly burned.

7. H_2O, or water, consists of two ______________________: hydrogen and oxygen.

8. Too much sun ______________________ can cause skin cancer. Be sure to use sunscreen.

Reading Skill

Understanding a Timeline

Timelines show the time order of events, such as important dates in history or in a person's life. Using a timeline can help you understand and remember information from a reading passage.

Look at the dates on the timeline. Go back to the reading passage on pages 155–156. Write information about Marie Curie's life on the timeline below in the box above or below the correct date.

The Life of Marie Curie

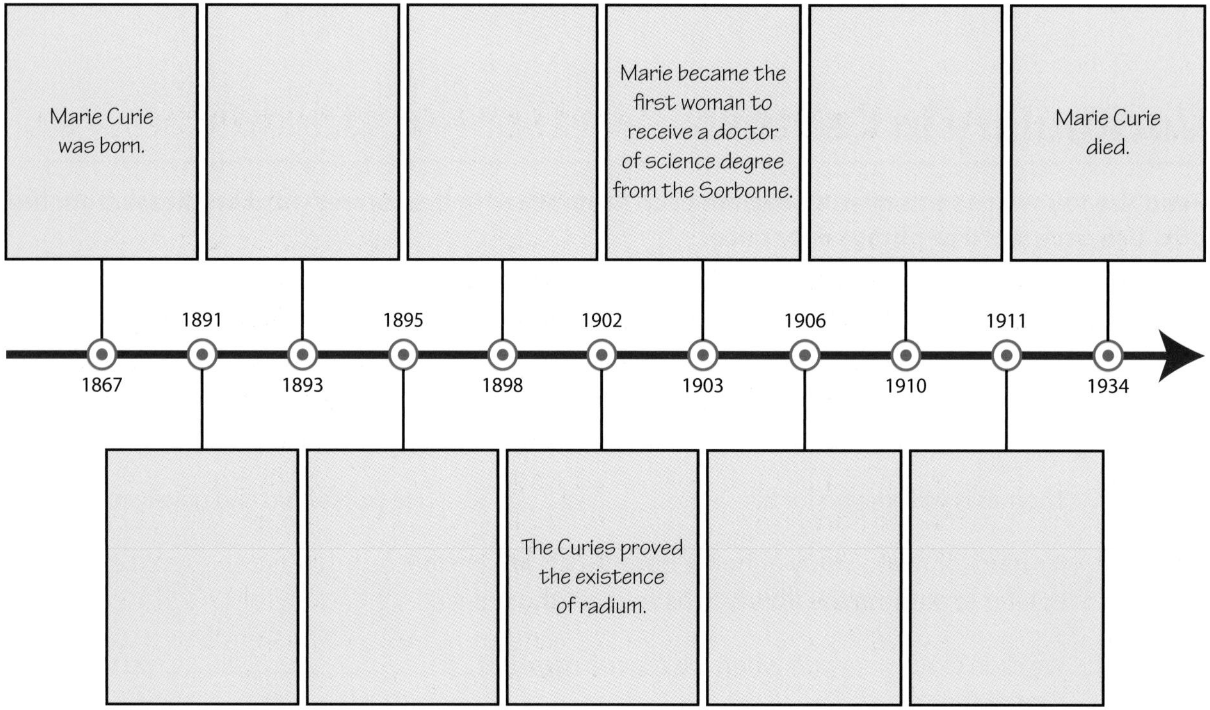

Irène Curie and her husband, Frédéric Joliot, who shared the Nobel Prize in 1935

Another Look

CD 2 TR 8 **Read the following passage about Irène Curie, Marie and Pierre Curie's daughter. Then answer the questions that follow.**

Irène Curie: Following in Her Mother's Footsteps

Most people are aware that Marie Curie was the first woman to win the Nobel Prize and the first person to win it twice. However, few people know that Marie Curie was also the mother of a Nobel Prize winner. Irène Curie was born on September 12, 1897. Irène was the first of Marie and Pierre Curie's two daughters. At the age of ten, Irène's talents and interest in mathematics were apparent. Irène, along with nine other children whose parents were also famous scholars, studied at their own school. It was known as the "Cooperative," and Marie Curie was one of their teachers. Irène finished her high school education at the College of Sévigné in Paris.

Irène entered the Sorbonne in October 1914 to prepare for a degree in mathematics and physics. When World War I began, Irène left the Sorbonne to assist her mother, who was using X-ray facilities to help save the lives of wounded soldiers. Irène continued this work by developing X-ray facilities in military hospitals in France and Belgium. After the war, Irène received a military medal for her work.

In 1918, Irène became her mother's assistant at the Curie Institute. In December 1924, Frédéric Joliot visited the institute, where he met Marie Curie. Frédéric became one of Marie's assistants, and Irène taught him the techniques required to work with radioactivity. Irène and Frédéric soon fell in love and were married on October 29, 1926. Their daughter, Hélène, was born on September 17, 1927, and their son, Pierre, on March 12, 1932. Like her mother, Irène successfully combined family and career. She was awarded a Nobel Prize, along with her husband Frédéric, in 1935, for synthesizing new radioactive elements. Unfortunately, also like her mother, Irène developed leukemia because of her exposure to radiation. She died from leukemia on March 17, 1956.

QUESTIONS FOR ANOTHER LOOK

1. How was Irène Curie's education unusual?

____

2. Where did Irène meet her husband?

____

3. Why did Irène receive a military medal for her work?

a. Because she did scientific research

b. Because she helped wounded soldiers

c. Because she received a degree in mathematics

4. Describe two ways that Irène and her mother, Marie Curie, were similar.

____

____

____

Marie Curie and her daughter, Irène

Topics for Discussion and Writing

1. Discuss these questions with a partner. Who wins Nobel Prizes? What types of work or discoveries deserve a Nobel Prize?

2. Marie Curie supported her sister Bronya when Bronya was in medical school. Then, when Bronya finished school, Marie began her own education. What kind of person do you think Marie was? Would you support your sister or brother if you could? Explain your reasons.

3. Marie Curie made a lot of sacrifices for her work. She never made any money from her discoveries, and she died as a result of her life's work: radium. Do you know of any other individuals who sacrificed their lives for their work? Do you think you could sacrifice your life for your work? Why or why not? Explain your reasons.

4. Write your autobiography or the biography of someone you know personally and who you admire.

5. Write in your journal. Work was the most important part of Marie Curie's life. Describe the most important part of your life at the present time. What do you think the most important part of your life will be in the future? Why?

Critical Thinking

1. Go online and search for more information about Marie and Pierre's younger daughter, Ève. For example, when was she born? What did she do? Was she a scientist, too? Did she become well known, too? Share your information with the class.

2. A biography is the story of a person's life. Prepare a biography of an important person from your country. Give an oral presentation to the class.

3. Work with a partner or in a small group. Make a list of the five most important discoveries of the 20th century. Remember, a discovery is something a person *finds*, something that already exists. An invention is something a person *creates*, such as the telephone, the light bulb, and the automobile. Share your list with your classmates. Then, as a class, choose the three most important discoveries.

4. Marie Curie postponed, or delayed, her own education for six years so her older sister Bronya could attend medical school. Why do you think she did this? Discuss this question with a partner.

5. What kind of woman was Marie Curie? Write some adjectives that describe her. Compare your list of adjectives with your classmates' lists.

6. Marie Curie never cared about making money. As a result, she sometimes worked under difficult conditions. Do you agree with her philosophy? Explain your reasons.

Crossword Puzzle

Review the words in the box. Then read the clues on the next page. Write the words in the correct spaces in the puzzle.

assist	field	once	support
constant	heartbroken	perseverance	tragic
discovery	interruption	radioactive	unfortunately
event	material	research	until
exposure			

Crossword Puzzle Clues

ACROSS CLUES

5. Pierre wanted to __________ Marie in her work, so he stopped working on his own.

6. Any long __________ to radioactivity can be very dangerous.

9. Marie didn't like any __________ when she was studying. She preferred to study alone.

11. Marie Curie lived in France __________ her death in 1934.

13. Marie decided to __________ her sister, Bronya, while Bronya was in medical school.

14. Scientific __________ on radioactive elements continues today.

16. Working with polonium and radium caused the Curies __________ illness.

17. The __________ of radium and polonium was very important to science.

DOWN CLUES

1. Element

2. The death of Pierre Curie was a terrible __________ in Marie Curie's life.

3. Radium and polonium are not the only __________ substances. There are many others.

4. Irène Curie and her husband were awarded the Nobel Prize in the __________ of chemistry.

7. The Curies did important work. __________, their work with radioactive materials made them sick.

8. When Pierre died, Marie was __________. It was very difficult for her.

10. Marie Curie's __________ was amazing. She never gave up.

12. The death of Pierre Curie at the age of 46 was a __________ accident.

15. Pierre began to help Marie __________ he realized she was doing very important work.

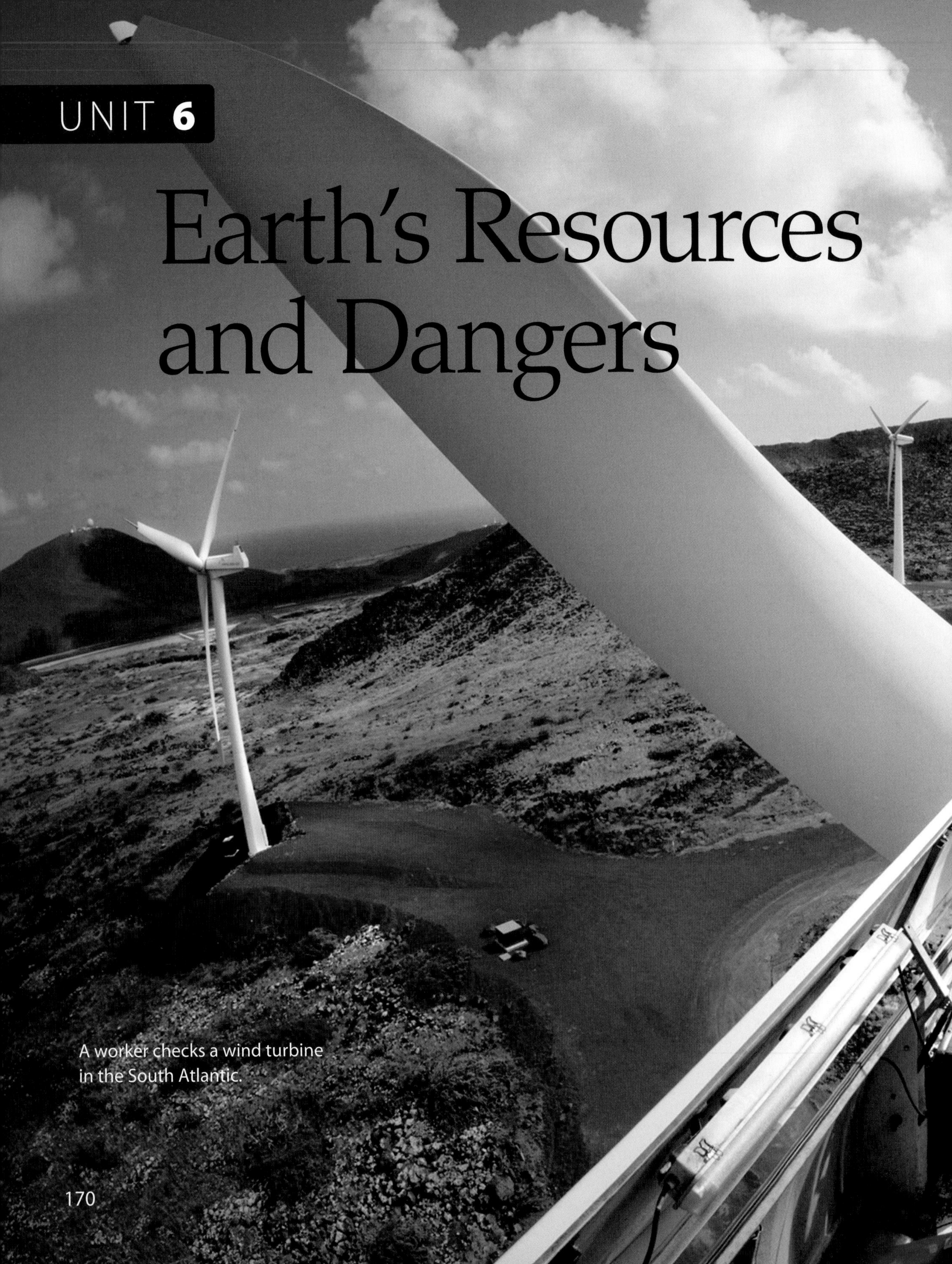

UNIT 6

Earth's Resources and Dangers

A worker checks a wind turbine in the South Atlantic.

1. What are some examples of natural disasters? Where do they occur?
2. What are some natural resources that are important to people's lives?

CHAPTER 11 Oil as an Important World Resource

Oil machinery in California

Prereading

Discuss these questions with a partner.

1. What are some uses of oil for the home and for transportation? Make a list in the chart below.

Uses of Oil	
Transportation	**Home**

2. Look at the illustration on page 174 and read the paragraph below. Then complete the flowchart using information from both.

The Formation of Oil

Oil is usually called petroleum. Petroleum is very complex, but it is made up of only two elements: carbon (C) and hydrogen (H). Together, carbon and hydrogen are called hydrocarbons. Hydrocarbons are the remains of ancient plants and animals. These plants and animals lived and died millions of years ago. When they died, mud covered them, and bacteria broke down the organic remains. Over thousands of years, more plants and animals died, and more mud covered them. The weight of the upper layers and the heat from the pressure eventually changed the mud into solid rock called sedimentary rock. It also changed the organic material into oil and natural gas.

FLOWCHART: THE FORMATION OF OIL

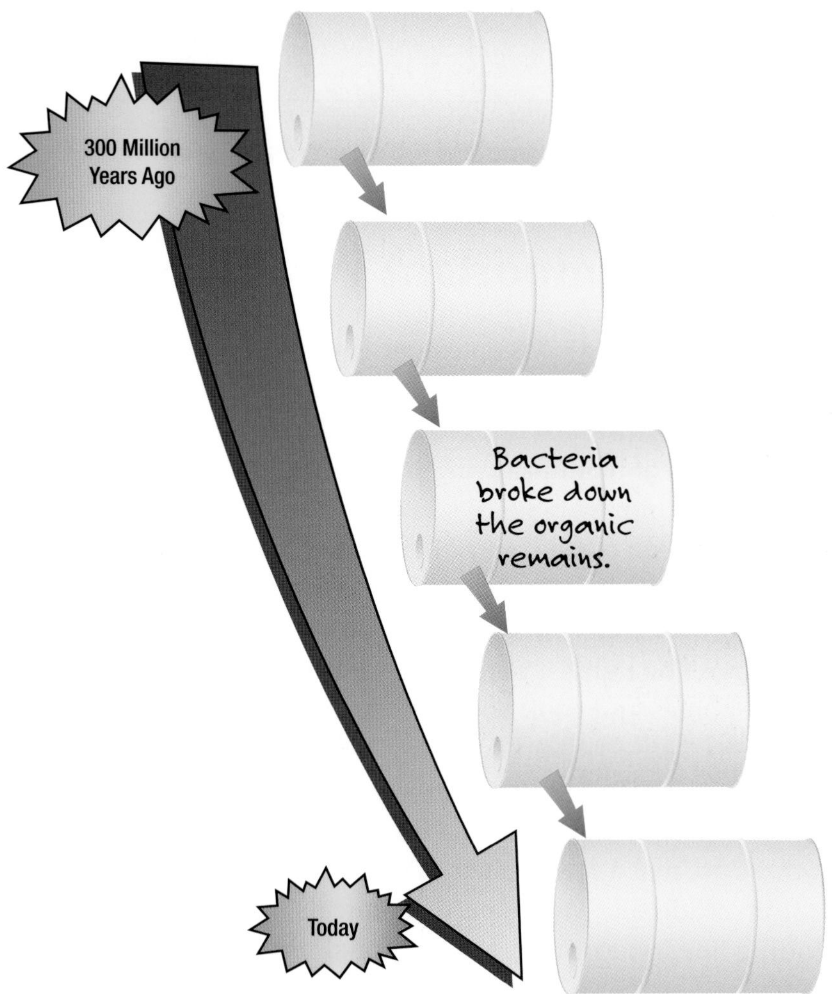

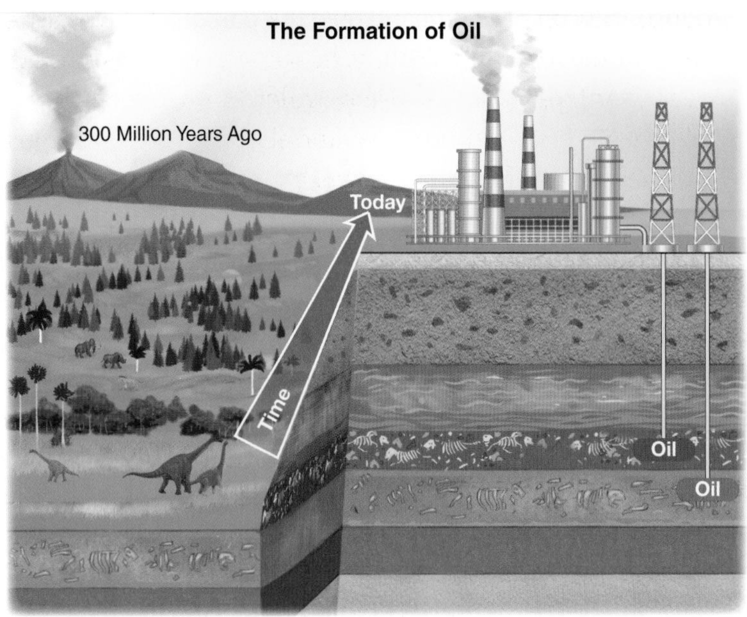

Reading

CD 2
TR 9

Read the passage carefully. Then complete the exercises that follow.

Oil as an Important World Resource

We may not realize it, but oil is an essential part of our everyday lives. Oil, or petroleum, is a valuable world resource. Many useful products come from it. In fact, petroleum is probably the most important substance we use in modern society, next to water. The process of manufacturing petroleum products begins when oil first comes out of the ground.

When petroleum first comes out of the ground, it is called crude oil. This oil is impure. In other words, it is dirty and people need to clean, or refine, it. First, the oil goes into a furnace that heats it. When the oil gets hot, it separates into lighter and heavier parts. The lightest part of the oil becomes natural gas. We use natural gas to heat our homes and cook with. The heaviest part of the oil becomes asphalt. We use asphalt to pave roads and parking lots. The process between the natural gas and the asphalt produces gasoline, kerosene, heating oil, and lubricating oil. We use lubricating oil to grease machines and other metal objects, for example, bicycles. However, these are just a few of the 6,000 petroleum products, or petrochemicals, that come from crude oil. We use petrochemicals in almost every area of our lives, including houses, clothing, and personal use, as well as medicine and transportation.

In the past, people's homes contained only natural materials, for example, wool or cotton carpets and wood furniture. Today, however, we use synthetic materials, such as rayon, nylon, and polyester. These are petroleum products. Our carpets, paint, and wallpaper usually come from synthetic materials, not natural materials.

We heat our homes with oil or natural gas instead of wood. Today, many of our clothes come from synthetic materials, too. We even make clothing from recycled plastic containers. We wash our dishes and clean our clothes with detergents. These are also petroleum products. Children's toys, shampoo, lipstick, and hand lotion are, too.

Petrochemicals have a wide variety of medical uses. Vitamins and some drugs that our doctors prescribe come from petrochemicals. For example, today's aspirin and other pain relievers such as acetaminophen are petrochemical products. Cold medicines that relieve our stuffy noses and drugs that help some people breathe more easily are petrochemicals, too.

The transportation industry depends on petrochemicals. We all know that gasoline, kerosene, and diesel oil provide fuel for cars, motorcycles, trucks, airplanes, and ships. However, not everyone is aware that cars and trucks are made of petrochemicals, too. For instance, car and truck bodies are made of hundreds of pounds of polyester. Bumpers are no longer made of steel, and tires are synthetic, not real, rubber. Seat covers are vinyl. Traffic lights, road signs, and the painted lines on roads are all petrochemicals.

The world's supply of petroleum may run out one day. However, we have an adequate supply for now. Petrochemical products will remain an essential part of our lives for many years to come.

Cars run on gasoline and are made of petrochemicals, too.

Fact Finding

Read the passage again. Then read the following statements. Check (√) whether each statement is True or False. If a statement is false, rewrite it so that it is true. Then go back to the passage and find the line that supports your answer.

1. _____ True _____ False Petroleum is another word for oil.

____

2. _____ True _____ False Crude oil does not need to be cleaned.

____

3. _____ True _____ False The lightest part of the oil becomes natural gas.

____

4. _____ True _____ False Kerosene is heavier than asphalt.

____

5. _____ True _____ False Our homes contain many products made of petrochemicals.

____

6. _____ True _____ False Petrochemicals have no medical uses.

____

7. _____ True _____ False We all use and depend on petroleum products.

____

Reading Analysis

Read each question carefully. Circle the letter or the number of the correct answer, or write your answer in the space provided.

1. Oil, or **petroleum**, is a valuable world resource. Many useful products come from it. **In fact**, petroleum is probably the most important substance we use in modern society, **next to** water.

a. What is a synonym for **petroleum**?

____

b. The sentence after **in fact**
   1. is the same as the sentence before it, but in different words.
   2. emphasizes the information before it.
   3. is a different idea from the information before it.

c. Complete the following sentence with the appropriate choice.
   Yesterday was a very cold day. **In fact**,
   1. I had to wear a heavy coat.
   2. it snowed all day long.
   3. the temperature was 10 degrees Fahrenheit below zero.

d. Petroleum is the most important substance we use in modern society, **next to** water.
   In modern society, which substance is the most important: petroleum or water?

   ____

2. When petroleum first comes out of the ground, it is called crude oil. This oil is **impure**. **In other words**, it is dirty and people need to clean, or **refine**, it.

a. **Impure** means
   1. oil.
   2. dirty.
   3. from the ground.

b. What type of information follows **in other words**?
   1. An example
   2. Additional information
   3. The same information in different words

c. What does **refine** mean?

   ____

d. How do you know?

   ____

3. We use lubricating oil to grease machines and other metal objects, for example, bicycles.

We use lubricating oil to grease bicycles

a. to keep air in the tires.
b. to help the brakes work well.
c. to keep them going smoothly.

4. We use **petrochemicals** in almost every area of our lives, including housing, clothing, and personal use, **as well as** medicine and transportation.

a. What are **petrochemicals**?

   ____

b. **As well as** means
   1. very good.
   2. equal to.
   3. in addition to.

5. In the past, people's homes contained only **natural** materials, for example, wool or cotton carpets and wood furniture. Today, however, we use **synthetic** materials, such as rayon, nylon, and polyester. These are petroleum products.

a. What are examples of **natural** materials?

____

b. **Synthetic** materials are
   1. artificial or man-made.
   2. materials for home use.

c. What are examples of **synthetic** materials?

____

6. We wash our dishes and clean our clothes with **detergents**. **These are petroleum products**. **Children's toys**, **shampoo**, **lipstick**, **and hand lotion are**, **too**.

a. **A detergent** is
   1. a kind of machine.
   2. a kind of soap.
   3. a kind of process.

b. The second and third sentences mean
   1. children's toys, shampoo, lipstick, and hand lotion are also petroleum-based products.
   2. children's toys, shampoo, lipstick, and hand lotion are also washed with detergents.

7. Vitamins and some drugs that our doctors **prescribe** come from petrochemicals. For example, today's aspirin and other pain **relievers** such as acetaminophen are petrochemical products.

a. When doctors **prescribe** medicine, they
   1. sell medicine to us.
   2. make medicine for us.
   3. order the use of a specific medicine.

b. A pain **reliever** is a drug that
   1. reduces our pain.
   2. increases our pain.

8. Car and truck **bodies** are made of hundreds of pounds of polyester.

Car and truck **bodies** are

a. people in cars and trucks.
b. the front, back, sides, and doors of cars and trucks.
c. the tires of cars and trucks.

9. **The world's supply of petroleum may run out one day.** However, we have an **adequate** supply for now.
   a. One day the world's supply of petroleum
      1. will be part of our lives.
      2. will not be necessary.
      3. might end.
   b. **Adequate** means
      1. expensive.
      2. enough.
      3. useful.

10. **Petrochemical products will remain an essential part of our lives for many years to come.**
    This sentence means that
    a. people don't need petrochemical products.
    b. people will need petrochemical products in the future.
    c. people will stop using petrochemical products in the future.

11. What is the main idea of this passage?
    a. Heating crude oil separates it into lighter and heavier parts.
    b. Petroleum is an essential natural resource that has many important uses.
    c. Petroleum is dirty when it comes from the ground and needs to be cleaned.

Vocabulary Skill

PART 1

Recognizing Word Forms

In English, some verbs become nouns by adding the suffix *-tion,* for example, *create (v.), creation (n.),* or *-ation,* for example, *inform (v), information (n.)* If the word ends in *e,* the *e* is dropped.

Complete each sentence with the correct word form on the left. Write all the verbs in the simple present. The nouns are all singular.

produce *(v.)*	**1.** The Middle East ________________ a lot of petroleum.
production *(n.)*	In fact, the oil ________________ in the Middle East is the highest in the world.

form *(v.)* **formation *(n.)***	**2.** The ______________________ of oil takes millions of years. Oil ______________________ over time from the remains of ancient plants and animals.
transport *(v.)* **transportation *(n.)***	**3.** The ______________________ of oil is done by pipeline, for example, in the state of Alaska. Petroleum companies ______________________ oil in large tankers, or ships.
lubricate *(v.)* **lubrication *(n.)***	**4.** Bike riders need to take good care of their bicycles. The ______________________ of the gears and the chain is important for bicycles. Careful bike riders ______________________ the gears and the chain of their bicycles regularly.
realize *(v.)* **realization *(n.)***	**5.** People ______________________ that the world's supply of petroleum may run out one day. Because of this ______________________, some companies are making cars that use electricity instead of gasoline.

PART 2

Understanding Synonyms

Synonyms are words with similar meanings. For example, *little* and *small* are synonyms.

Match each word with its synonym. Write the letter of the correct answer and the word or phrase on the line provided.

b. know about	1. aware of	a. divide
____________	2. essential	~~b. know about~~
____________	3. important	c. man-made
____________	4. manufacture	d. material
____________	5. process	e. method
____________	6. separate	f. necessary
____________	7. substance	g. produce
____________	8. synthetic	h. valuable

Vocabulary in Context

Read the following sentences. Complete each sentence with the correct word or phrase from the box. Use each word or phrase only once.

adequate *(adj.)*	fuel *(n.)*	next to	substance *(n.)*
as well as	impure *(adj.)*	process *(n.)*	synthetic *(adj.)*

1. Gasoline and kerosene are two types of ________________.
2. Grease is a very oily ________________. You need a strong detergent to wash it off your hands.
3. Don't drink any water from that river. It is ________________. Drink the bottled water you have with you instead.
4. Making good coffee is a very simple ________________. All you need is fresh, cold water and the right amount of coffee.
5. There is an ________________ number of desks for all the students in this class. We don't need any more desks.
6. Today, many objects are made of ________________ materials. Many of these materials come from petrochemicals.
7. I read books for pleasure ________________ for information. Both are important to me.
8. ________________ chocolate cake, my favorite dessert is ice cream.

Reading Skill

Understanding Bar Graphs

Bar graphs often show percentages. Learning how to read bar graphs can help you understand important information from the reading passage.

Look at the bar graph below and answer the questions.

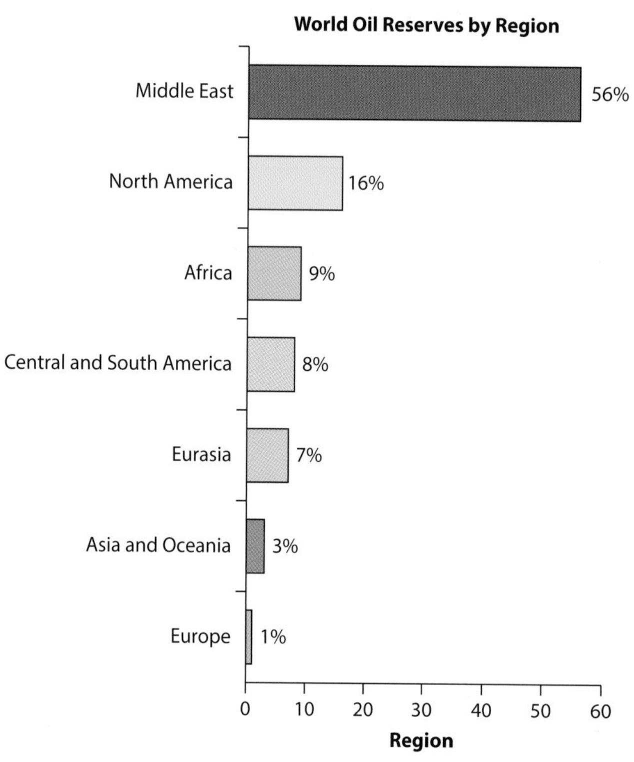

a. Which region has the largest oil reserves in the world?

____

b. Which region has the smallest oil reserves in the world?

____

c. Which region has the second-largest oil reserves in the world?

____

d. Which one of the following statements is true?

1. The Middle East has smaller oil reserves than all the other countries and areas combined.
2. The Middle East has the same amount of oil reserves as all of the other countries and areas combined.
3. The Middle East has bigger oil reserves than all of the other countries and regions combined.

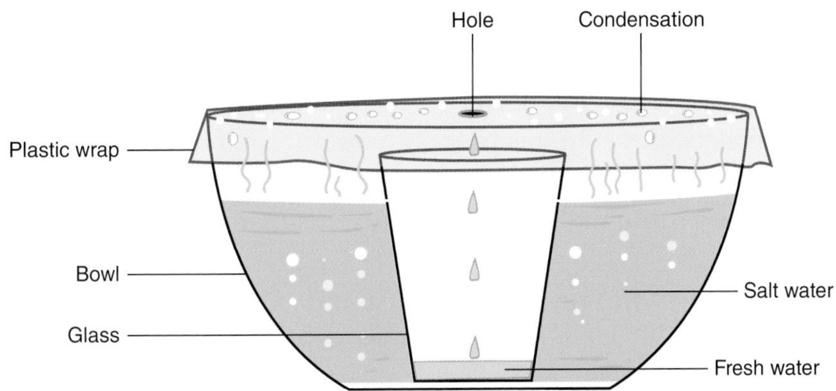

Another Look

Read the following passage about the world's need for fresh water. Then answer the questions that follow.

CD 2 TR 10

Fresh Water for the World

Everyone knows that people need water to live, and there's a lot of water on Earth. In fact, water covers about 70 percent of the earth's surface. Most of that water is in the oceans. However, ocean water is salty, so we can't drink it. We need to drink fresh water, which comes from lakes and rivers. However, only three percent of the earth's water is fresh water. Furthermore, many people do not have access to fresh water because they live near oceans. How can people solve this problem of access? One solution is to turn salt water into fresh water. Desalination is the process of taking the salt out of ocean water and turning it into fresh water.

The process of desalination seems simple. Children sometimes learn about it in elementary school science classes. To do it, simply fill a large bowl with salt water and put an empty glass in the middle. Then cover the bowl and the empty glass with plastic wrap. Make a small hole in the middle of the plastic wrap and put the bowl, glass, and water in the sun. When the salt water evaporates, it leaves the salt behind and creates condensation. The condensation rises to the plastic wrap and drips into the empty glass. The water in the glass is now fresh water and is good enough to drink. Although this is a simple process, it is often very expensive to do for large amounts of water.

The first desalination method was similar to the simple process above: Heat seawater until it turns to steam and leaves its salt behind (see diagram below). However, this process uses a lot of energy. Today, the most common method of removing salt from seawater is reverse osmosis. In this process, you put salt water on one side of a filter. Pressure moves the water through the filter. The salt cannot pass through the filter, but fresh water can pass through to the other side. This method uses less energy, but it is still expensive.

People all over the world need fresh water, and every year they need more. As technology develops, we will find less expensive ways to desalinate water. We will be able to bring fresh water to the people who need it most.

How Sea Water Becomes Fresh Water

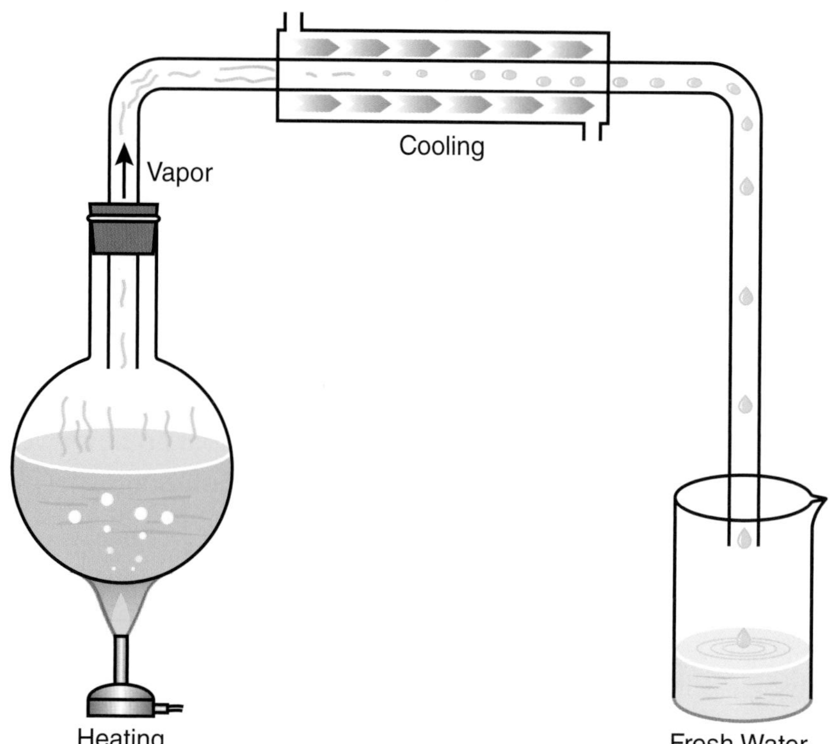

QUESTIONS FOR ANOTHER LOOK

1. Look at the diagram on the previous page. Find the sentence in the reading that describes this picture. Write the sentence on the lines below.

   ____

   ____

2. Where is most of the world's water? Can people drink it?

   ____

3. Why can't many people get fresh water?

   ____

4. What is desalination?

   ____

   ____

5. Why are most desalination processes expensive?

   ____

   ____

Topics for Discussion and Writing

1. Think about people's lives at home, at work, at school, and so on. Describe how oil makes life easier for people.

2. The first reading passage explains the process of changing oil into different products. Think of another process where something is changed into a useful product. Describe the process, for example, of how people change wood into paper.

3. There are many other scientific advances that make life better or easier for us. Work with a classmate and make a list. Then select one of the advances and describe it.

4. Write in your journal. Imagine there is no more oil in the world. Describe a day in your life without oil.

An oil refinery

Critical Thinking

1. Make a list in the chart below of the ways you use petrochemical products in your life. When you are finished, compare your list with a classmate's list. What products did you list that were not mentioned in the passage?

My Uses of Petroleum-Based Products					
Housing	**Clothing**	**Personal Uses**	**Medical Uses**	**Transportation**	**Other Uses**

2. Are there other ways to remove salt from water? Go online. Find information about another desalination process and report it to the class.

3. Refer to the illustration on page 183. Try the desalination process that some children learn about in elementary school. How long does the process take? Who do you think this process may be useful for?

4. Besides oil, what is another valuable natural resource that is essential to our lives? Why is this natural resource essential? Compare your answer with your classmates' answers.

5. How do you think everyday life in the past was different without oil? Was it easier or more difficult? Explain your answer and give examples.

6. What are other sources of energy that people can use instead of oil? Look for information about this energy source online. Present your information to your classmates.

Crossword Puzzle

Review the words in the box. Then read the clues on the next page. Write the words in the correct spaces in the puzzle.

adequate	manufacture	prescribe	separates
aware	natural	process	substance
detergent	petrochemicals	refine	synthetic
essential	petroleum	reliever	valuable
impure			

1 2 3 4 5 6 7 8 9 10 11 12 13 14 15 16

Crossword Puzzle Clues

ACROSS CLUES

1. Oil __________ into lighter and heavier parts when it is heated.
3. Another word for oil is __________.
5. __________ means unclean or dirty.
7. A pain __________ such as acetaminophen is made from oil.
8. Are you __________ that traffic lights and road signs are actually made of oils and chemicals?
10. Asphalt, kerosene, and gas are some of the products that people __________ from crude oil.
12. The __________ of cleaning crude oil and making other products from it takes time.
13. Water is the most important __________ in our lives, but oil is important, too.
14. We use __________ to clean our clothes.
15. Cotton and wool are __________ fibers.
16. Nylon is a __________ fiber. It is man-made.

DOWN CLUES

2. People need to __________, or clean, oil after it comes out of the ground.
3. __________ are oil-based products.
4. Oil and gas are __________ natural resources. They are very important to our everyday lives.
6. Doctors often __________ drugs that are made from oil.
9. The world's reserves of oil and gas are __________ for now. However, one day they will run out.
11. Air and water are __________ to our lives. We can't live without them.

CHAPTER 12 Earthquakes: Powerful and Deadly

A man walks through buildings that were destroyed in the Van-Erics earthquake in Turkey.

Prereading

Discuss these questions with a partner.

1. Where in the world do earthquakes occur? Do they occur in your country?
2. What kinds of damage do earthquakes cause?
3. How do earthquakes happen?

A seismograph station in Bergisch Gladbach, Germany.

Reading

CD 2 TR 11 **Read the following passage carefully. Then answer the questions that follow.**

Earthquakes: Powerful and Deadly

Earthquake! People all around the world fear earthquakes because they cause so much destruction and death. Consider the following facts: an earthquake occurred near the East Coast of Honshu, Japan, on March 11, 2011. The earthquake caused 20,896 deaths, over 6,000 injuries, and extensive building damage. Even worse, the earthquake caused a tsunami, which is a series of huge powerful waves that spread quickly over land. The March 2011 tsunami damaged a nuclear power plant, which affected hundreds of thousands of people. In fact, the March 2011 earthquake ranks as the most powerful earthquake that ever struck Japan.

On December 26, 2004, an earthquake took place off the West Coast of Northern Sumatra. This underwater earthquake resulted in a tsunami that caused over 230,000 deaths and billions of dollars in damage. The Sumatra earthquake was the third largest earthquake in history since 1900.

These statistics are very frightening. Many people who live in areas where earthquakes are possible worry about the risk of earthquakes and tsunamis. However, these people can receive more news and information now because of improved world communication. For example, in the last 20 years, scientists have been able to locate more earthquakes annually because there are more seismograph, or earthquake-measuring, stations in the world. These stations help locate many small earthquakes that scientists couldn't detect years ago.

Many scientists are trying to predict earthquakes and tsunamis, too, but these predictions are very uncertain. Scientists cannot calculate the exact location, time, or intensity of an earthquake. Furthermore, the predicted earthquake may not take place at all. As a result, scientists do not think it is useful to announce that an earthquake will take place on a specific day. Instead, many people are trying to design structures such as buildings, dams, and bridges that can resist earthquakes and tsunamis. People can reduce the number of deaths, injuries, and the amount of property damage by preparing themselves, their homes, and their work places for major earthquakes. After all, it is possible to survive an earthquake.

Fact Finding

Read the passage again. Then read the following statements. Check (√) whether each statement is True or False. If a statement is false, rewrite it so that it is true. Then go back to the passage and find the line that supports your answer.

1. ____ True ____ False The earthquake in Japan caused more deaths than the earthquake in Sumatra.

____

2. ____ True ____ False The March 2011 earthquake ranks as the most powerful earth-quake in the world.

____

3. ____ True ____ False People can receive more news and information about earthquakes because of improved world communication.

____

4. ____ True ____ False Scientists can predict the exact location of an earthquake before it occurs.

____

5. _____ True _____ False We can protect ourselves from earthquakes.

____

6. _____ True _____ False It's impossible to survive an earthquake.

____

Reading Analysis

Read each question carefully. Circle the letter or the number of the correct answer, or write your answer in the space provided.

1. **Consider** the following facts: an earthquake occurred near the East Coast of Honshu, Japan, on March 11, 2011. The earthquake caused 20,896 deaths, **over 6,000 injuries**, and **extensive** building damage.

a. **Consider** means
   1. think about.
   2. remember.
   3. be afraid of.

b. **Over 6,000 injuries** means
   1. exactly 6,000 people were hurt.
   2. more than 6,000 people were hurt.
   3. fewer than 6,000 people were hurt.

c. **Extensive** means
   1. a little.
   2. a lot of.
   3. expensive.

2. **Even worse**, the earthquake caused a **tsunami**, which is a series of huge powerful waves that spread quickly over land. The March 2011 tsunami **damaged** a nuclear power plant, which affected hundreds of thousands of people. **In fact**, the March 2011 earthquake **ranks** as the most powerful earthquake that ever struck Japan.

a. **Even worse** means
   1. the tsunami was worse than the earthquake.
   2. the earthquake was worse than the tsunami.

b. A **tsunami** is
   1. a kind of earthquake.
   2. a series of huge waves.

c. **Damage** means
   1. harm or break.
   2. cost a lot.
   3. protect.

d. What information follows **in fact**?
   1. Different information that introduces a new idea
   2. Additional information that gives more details about the previous sentence
   3. True information that everyone believes

e. How does the March 2011 earthquake **rank** as a natural disaster in Japan?
   1. It was very bad, but not the worst.
   2. It was the worst.

f. When we **rank** something, we
   a. classify it in order of importance.
   b. describe it as a natural occurrence.
   c. date it as a recent occurrence.

3. **These statistics** are very frightening.

What are **these statistics**?

a. The number of earthquakes that happen every year in Sumatra and Japan
b. The number of people who died in earthquakes in the last few years in Sumatra and Japan
c. The number of deaths and injuries, and the amount of damage from the earthquakes in Sumatra and Japan

4. In the last 20 years, scientists have been able to **locate** more earthquakes yearly because there are more **seismograph**, or earthquake-measuring, **stations** in the world.

a. **Locate** means
   1. predict.
   2. find.
   3. build.

b. What does a **seismograph station** do?

____

5. These stations help locate many small earthquakes that scientist couldn't **detect** years ago.

Detect means
a. notice or see.
b. understand.
c. prevent.

6. Many scientists are trying to **predict** earthquakes and tsunamis, too, but these predictions are very uncertain. Scientists cannot **calculate** the exact location, time, or intensity of an earthquake. **Furthermore**, the predicted earthquake may not take place at all.

a. **Predict** means
   1. stop something from happening.
   2. tell something will happen before it happens.
   3. understand something by reading about it.

b. **Calculate** means
   1. tell everyone.
   2. see.
   3. figure out.

c. What information comes after **furthermore**?
   1. More information about the same subject
   2. The same information in different words
   3. The result of the information before "furthermore"

7. **As a result**, scientists do not think it is a useful idea to announce that an earthquake will take place on a specific day.

a. Why don't scientists think it is a useful idea to announce that an earthquake will take place?
   1. Because they don't want people to protect themselves
   2. Because they are not sure what time the earthquake will occur
   3. Because the predicted earthquake might not take place at all

b. Complete the second sentence with the correct choice.
   Elizabeth read several interesting books about earthquakes. **As a result**,
   1. she became a better reader.
   2. she decided to live in California.
   3. she learned many new facts about earthquakes.

c. **As a result** means
   1. moreover.
   2. consequently.
   3. however.

8. **Instead**, many people are trying to design structures such as buildings, dams, and bridges that can **resist** earthquakes and tsunamis.

a. **Instead** introduces an idea that
   1. is similar to the previous idea.
   2. gives more details about the previous idea.
   3. takes the place of the previous idea.

b. A building that can **resist** an earthquake
   1. will fall down.
   2. will not fall down.

9. What is the main idea of this reading?

a. Earthquakes, which occur all over the world, cause deaths, injuries, and destruction, and they are very difficult to predict.

b. Earthquakes occur all over the world, but we can protect ourselves if we are prepared.

c. There are many seismological centers all over the world that can tell us when an earthquake will occur.

Vocabulary Skills

PART 1

Recognizing Word Forms

In English, some verbs become nouns by adding the suffix *-ment,* for example, *improve (v.), improvement (n.).*

Complete each sentence with the correct word form on the left. Write all the verbs in the simple present. The nouns may be singular or plural.

move *(v.)* **movement *(n.)***	1. The ____________ of the earth during an earthquake can be very fast. Buildings and bridges ____________ and cause a lot of damage.
place *(v.)* **placement *(n.)***	2. Scientists ____________ seismograph stations around the world. The ____________ of these stations helps locate many small earthquakes.
announce *(v.)* **announcement *(n.)***	3. Scientists do not think it's a good idea to ____________ that an earthquake will take place. This ____________ may be wrong because scientists are not sure when an earthquake will occur.
measure *(v.)* **measurement *(n.)***	4. Many scientists ____________ the strength of an earthquake with a Richter scale. The Richter scale's ____________ ranges from 1 to 10, with 10 being the most intense.
require *(v.)* **requirement *(n.)***	5. Some cities have ____________ for all new buildings and bridges. They ____________ that all new buildings and bridges are strong enough to resist earthquakes.

PART 2

Understanding Antonyms

Antonyms are words that have opposite meanings. For example, *old* and *young* are antonyms.

Match each word with its antonym. Write the letter of the correct answer and the word on the line provided.

g. result	1. cause	a. die
______	2. damage	b. increase
______	3. locate	c. hopeless
______	4. major	d. lose
______	5. possible	e. minor
______	6. reduce	f. repair
______	7. survive	~~g. result~~
______	8. useful	h. useless

Vocabulary in Context

Read the following sentences. Complete each sentence with the correct word or phrase from the box. Use each word or phrase only once.

as a result	locate *(v.)*	requirement *(n.)*	surface *(n.)*
calculate *(v.)*	predict *(v.)*	statistics *(n.)*	survive *(v.)*

1. Isabella used the GPS on her cell phone to ______________ the art museum in her new city.

2. Good eyesight is a ______________ for an airline pilot. You need to be able to see well in order to fly a plane.

3. A human being cannot ______________ without water for more than a week.

4. Can you help me ______________ how many miles per gallon I will get from my car? I want to know how much gas I will need for my trip.

5. No one knows exactly when an earthquake will occur. No one can ________________ when a volcano will erupt, either.

6. The ________________ of the moon has no water. However, there may be frozen water underneath.

7. According to ________________, more than 30,000 earthquakes occurred in 2008. This number is higher than the number of earthquakes in 2007.

8. Greg forgot his house keys. ________________, he couldn't get into his home until his father returned from work.

Reading Skill

Using an Illustration and Text to Create a Flowchart

Sometimes illustrations accompany a text to make the text easier to understand. Using both illustrations and text to create a flowchart can help you understand information better.

CD 2 TR 12 **Look at the illustration. It shows four different ways that earthquakes occur. Read the paragraph on the next page. Using information from both the paragraph and the illustration, fill in the flowchart on page 199.**

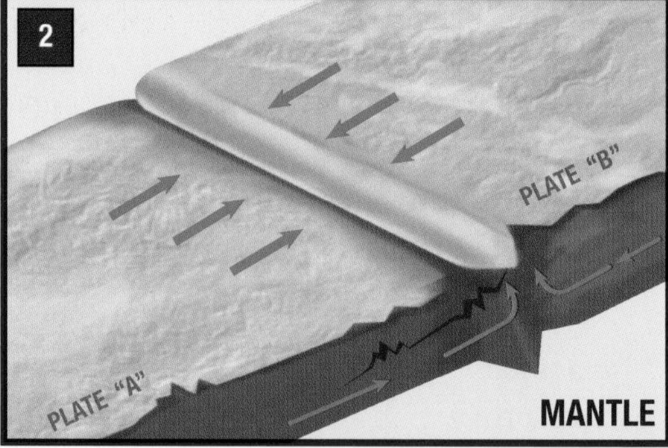

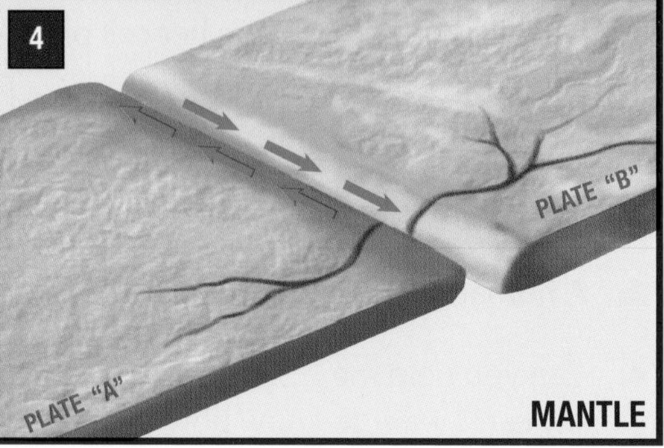

How Earthquakes Occur

The earth's crust, or surface, is made of rock. The crust covers the earth, but it is not in one piece. It is broken into a number of large pieces called plates. These plates are always moving because they lie on top of liquid rock. They slide over the hot, melted rock. The plates move very slowly in different directions. The difference in motion causes the earth's crust to break. This is an earthquake. Earthquakes happen in different ways. In some areas of the earth, the plates move apart. This happens in the middle of the Atlantic Ocean. Earthquakes also take place inside of plates throughout the world. For example, China is being squeezed in two directions, from the east by the Pacific plate and from the south by the Indo-Australian plate.

In other places, plates push directly against each other, and one plate moves downward under the other plate. For instance, this happens off the western coasts of South and Central America and off the coast of Japan. The plates are sliding past one another in other regions of the world, for example, in the San Andreas Fault Zone in California.

How Earthquakes Occur

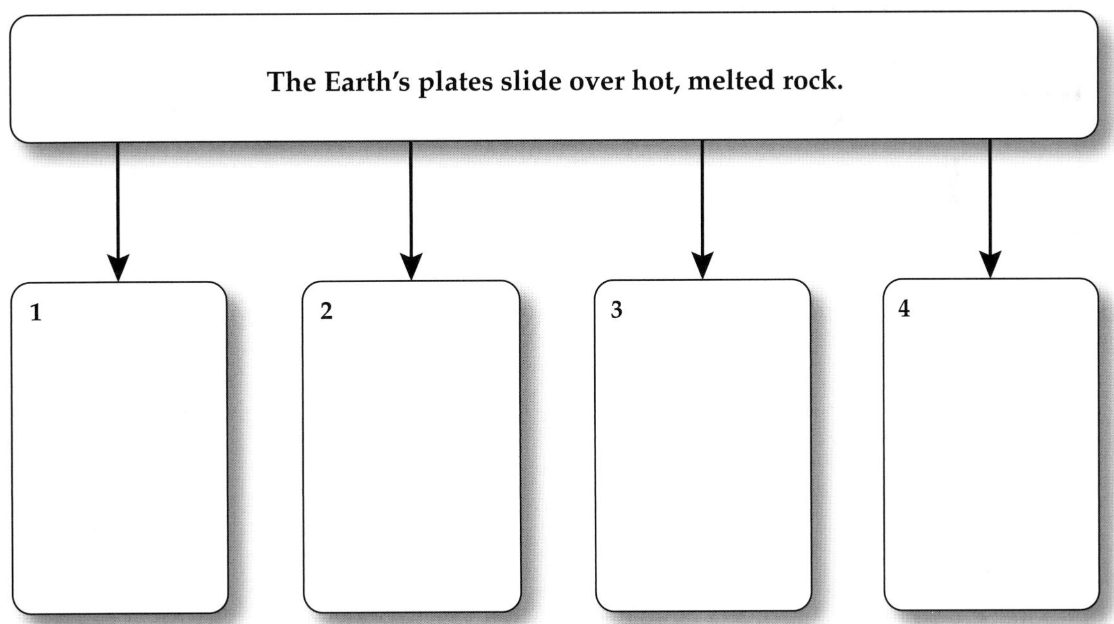

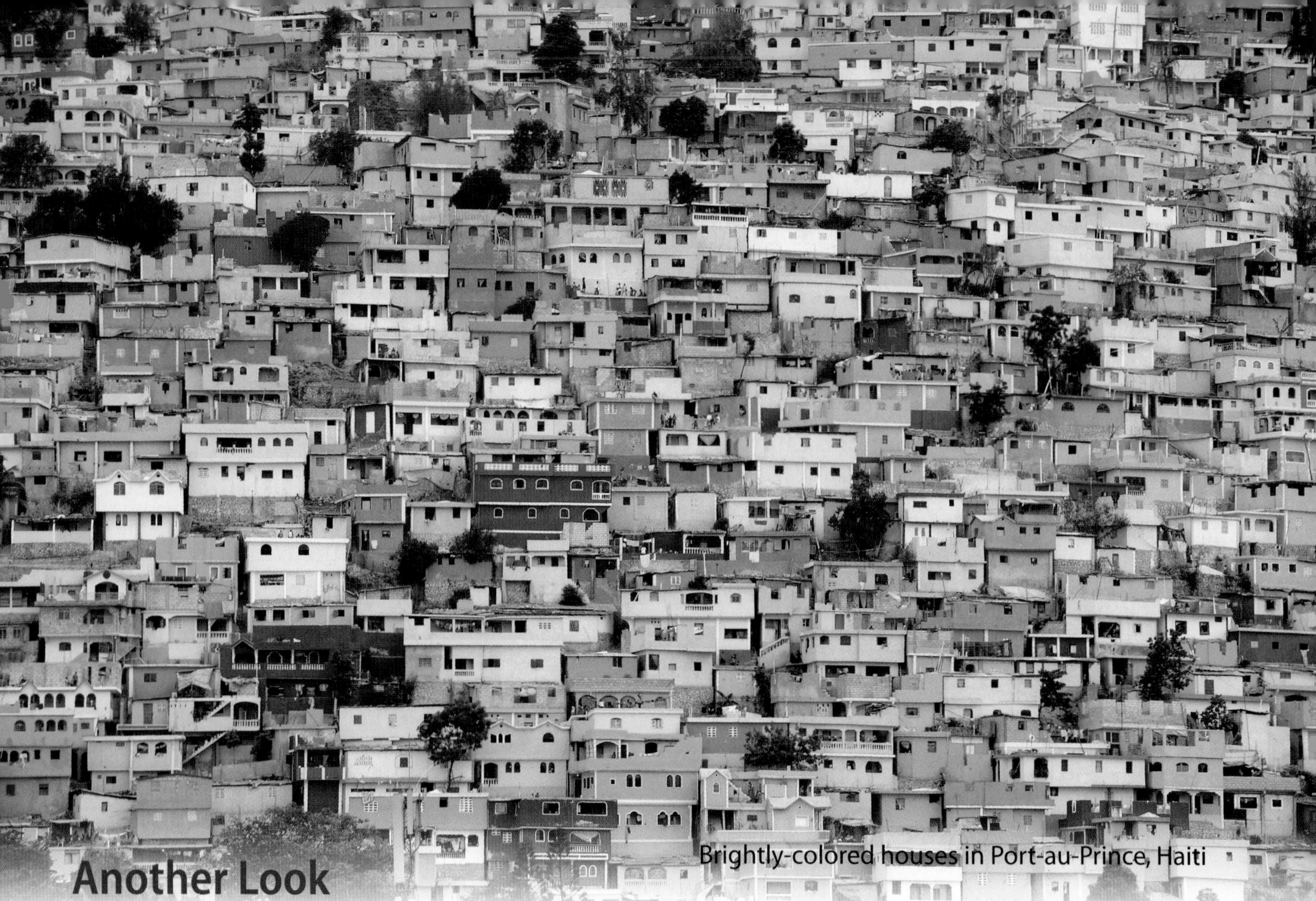
Brightly-colored houses in Port-au-Prince, Haiti

Another Look

CD 2 TR 13

Read the passage about an earthquake survivor. Then answer the questions that follow.

A Survivor's Story

My name is Marie, and I live in Port-au-Prince, Haiti. There were no major earthquakes in our country for over 60 years. The one that occurred on January 12, 2010, took all of us by surprise.

My son's family and I live in a small house in Port-au-Prince. When the earthquake began, it was afternoon. The movement threw me onto the floor. I wanted to get to my son and his wife in another room, but I couldn't—the amount of movement in our home was incredible. The door near where I was standing was swinging back and forth. I listened helplessly while just about everything standing in our home fell over. Loose objects flew across rooms while the shaking continued. The noise was incredibly loud. When the earthquake finally stopped, I hurried to find my son and his family. Then we looked around our home. It was badly damaged. All the windows were broken. In the kitchen, most of the dishes lay in small pieces all across the kitchen floor.

Outside, we saw that our neighbors' houses were badly damaged, too. People were standing near their homes, and everyone looked shocked and frightened. Many people were killed or injured.

Although we were all safe, we were still very affected by a terrible fear. In addition, we lost electrical power and had no water. It was a terrifying experience, and everyone in our country struggled to rebuild our homes and our lives. We love our beautiful city of Port-au-Prince, and we do not want to leave it. We hope this never happens again.

QUESTIONS FOR ANOTHER LOOK

1. Marie says, "There were no major earthquakes in our country for over 60 years. The one that occurred on January 12, 2010, took all of us by surprise."
   Why were Marie and her family surprised by the earthquake?
   a. Her family lived in Haiti for over 60 years.
   b. Haiti has a lot of major earthquakes.
   c. There were no major earthquakes in Haiti during her family's lifetime.

2. Why was the noise incredibly loud during the earthquake?

   ____

   ____

3. What kind of damage did Marie's home have after the earthquake?

   ____

   ____

4. Do you think Marie's family will continue to live in Port-au-Prince? Why or why not?

   ____

   ____

Topics for Discussion and Writing

1. If you know someone who experienced an earthquake, interview that person. Then write a composition describing the person's experience.

2. Work in a group of three. Imagine that an earthquake took place an hour ago. Your team must organize a rescue in your classroom building. Decide what things you have to do. List these actions in their order of importance. Then assign responsibilities to each member of your group. Have each group member write a composition describing his or her plan of action.

3. Imagine that you are a teacher. Prepare a set of instructions for your students. Tell them what to do if an earthquake occurs.

4. Write in your journal. Imagine that an earthquake took place where you live. Describe the experience. What happened immediately before the earthquake? What happened during the earthquake? What happened after the earthquake? What did you think about? How did you feel?

Critical Thinking

1. A seismograph is an instrument that scientists use to locate and record earthquakes. Scientists measure the energy, or intensity, of earthquakes with a Richter scale. The Richter scale measures the intensity, or strength, of earthquakes on a scale of 1 to 10, with 10 being the most intense. Work in a group. Look at the map below and read the list of earthquakes around the world on the next page. Write the number in the circle that indicates the location of each earthquake.

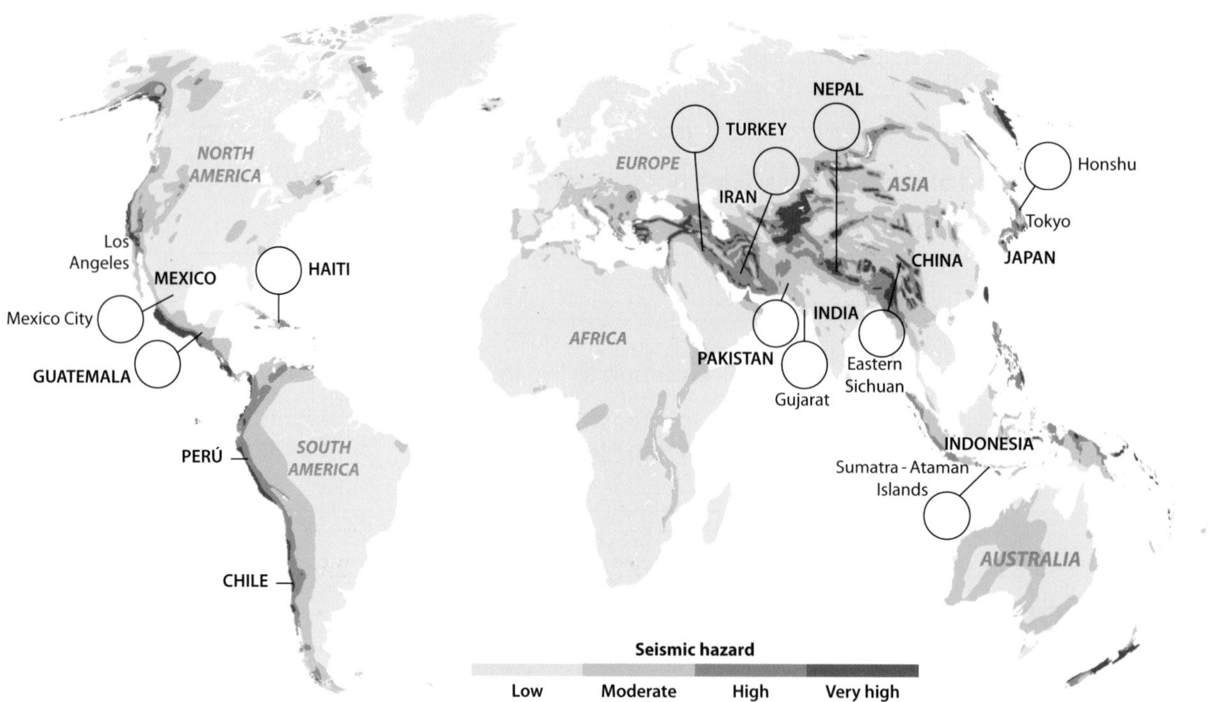

2. Look at the chart below and answer the questions that follow.

Deadly Earthquakes around the World			
Location	**Date**	**Intensity on Richter Scale**	**Number of Deaths**
1. Guatemala	Feb. 1976	7.5	23,000
2. Mexico City	Sep. 1985	8.1	9,000
3. Eastern Turkey	Mar. 1992	6.2	4,000
4. Gujarat, India	Jan. 2001	7.6	20,000
5. Southeastern Iran	Dec. 2003	6.6	13,000
6. Sumatra-Andaman Islands	Dec. 2004	9.1	228,000
7. Pakistan	Oct. 2005	7.6	86,000
8. Eastern Sichuan, China	May 2008	7.9	88,000
9. Haiti	Jan. 2010	7.0	315,000
10. Honshu, Japan	Mar. 2011	9.0	15,000
11. Nepal	Apr. 2015	7.8	8,000

a. Where was the earthquake with the highest intensity on the Richter scale?

____

b. Where were the most people killed in an earthquake?

____

c. Why were so many people killed there? What do you think?

____

d. In some places, earthquakes kill fewer than 1,000 people, while in other places many thousands of people die. What might be some reasons why more people are killed in some places than in others? What do you think?

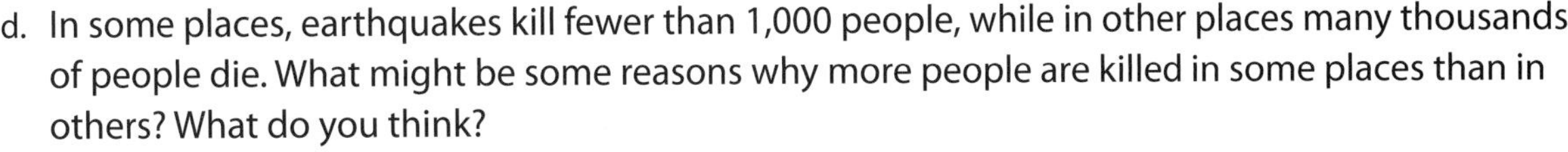

____

____

3. Read the following checklist for home safety during an earthquake.

Prepare Your Home for an Earthquake

❑ 1. Make sure that hanging lights are not above beds.

❑ 2. Make sure that beds are not right below heavy mirrors.

❑ 3. Make sure that beds are not right below framed pictures.

❑ 4. Make sure that beds are not right below shelves with lots of objects that can fall.

❑ 5. Make sure that beds are not next to large windows.

❑ 6. Take all heavy objects off high shelves.

❑ 7. Take all breakable objects off high shelves.

❑ 8. Make sure that heavy mirrors are well fastened to walls.

❑ 9. Make sure that heavy pictures are well fastened to walls.

❑ 10. Make sure that air conditioners are well supported in windows.

4. Work in a group. Look at the bedroom in the photo below. Decide how to make the bedroom safer in the event of an earthquake. Refer to the checklist above. When you are finished, compare your ideas with another group's.

5. It is important to know what to do during an earthquake. Read the following list. In pairs, decide what to do and what not to do during an earthquake. When you finish, compare your list with another pair of students. Be prepared to give reasons for your decisions.

_____ Yes _____ No a. Stay calm and don't do anything to upset other people.

_____ Yes _____ No b. Run to other rooms and shout, "Earthquake! Earthquake!"

_____ Yes _____ No c. If you are indoors, get under a desk or a table, if possible.

_____ Yes _____ No d. If you are in a high building, take the elevator to the first floor.

_____ Yes _____ No e. If you are inside a building, do not run outside.

_____ Yes _____ No f. If you are outside near a building, stand in a doorway.

_____ Yes _____ No g. If you are outside, but not near a building, try to get into an open area away from buildings and power lines.

_____ Yes _____ No h. If you are in a car, continue driving to get as far away from the earthquake as possible.

_____ Yes _____ No i. If the electrical power lines and gas lines break, use matches and candles for light.

_____ Yes _____ No j. If you are in an empty room with no desk or table, stand in a doorway.

6. Certain areas of the world experience earthquakes often, especially places such as Japan and Sumatra. Why do you think people continue to live where earthquakes are likely to take place? Discuss this question with your classmates.

7. Scientists do not think it is a good idea to announce an earthquake because it may not actually take place. Do you agree with the scientists? Explain your answer.

8. Think of another natural disaster that people need to prepare themselves for. Go online and find information about it. How can people prepare for this kind of natural disaster? Present your information to your class.

Crossword Puzzle

Review the words in the box. Then read the clues on the next page. Write the words in the correct spaces in the puzzle.

calculate	even	instead	resist
consider	extensive	locate	seismographic
damage	fact	predict	statistics
detect	furthermore	ranks	tsunami

Crossword Puzzle Clues

ACROSS CLUES

2. There are many __________ instruments all over the world. They measure the intensity of earthquakes.

5. Today, scientists can __________ smaller earthquakes than they could years ago.

10. Scientists are able to __________ more earthquakes every year. It's very important to know where they occur.

11. I want to live in California, but I am afraid of earthquakes. I will live in Colorado __________.

12. The number of deaths and injuries caused by earthquakes are very frightening __________.

14. We need to construct buildings that can __________ earthquakes.

15. The earthquake that occurred in 1556 in Shensi, China, __________ as the deadliest earthquake in history: 830,000 people died.

16. When the earthquake occurred in my city, I lost my home. __________, I lost my job because my business was destroyed, too.

DOWN CLUES

1. It takes time to __________ how much it will cost to rebuild after an earthquake occurs.

3. Earthquakes make buildings fall and break up roads. __________ worse, they cause deaths and injuries.

4. Unfortunately, scientists cannot __________ exactly when an earthquake will occur.

6. Some earthquakes cause many deaths. In __________, they sometimes cause hundreds of thousands of deaths.

7. Often, a __________ causes even more deaths, injuries, and destruction than an earthquake.

8. A recent earthquake caused millions of dollars in __________ to homes and businesses.

9. A major earthquake always requires __________ rebuilding because so many buildings, bridges, and roads need to be replaced.

13. People need to __________ the dangers of living near an area where earthquakes occur.

INDEX OF KEY WORDS AND PHRASES

Words with AWL beside them are on the Academic Words List (AWL), Coxhead (2000). The AWL is a list of the 570 highest-frequency academic word families that regularly appear in academic texts. Researcher Avril Coxhead compiled this list from a corpus of 3.5 million words.

SKILLS INDEX

GRAMMAR AND USAGE

LISTENING/SPEAKING

READING

TOPICS

VISUAL LITERACY

WRITING

CREDITS

Cover: Lucerne Festival ARK NOVA

iii (t) [Reading for Today], used courtesy of North Carolina State University, Raleigh, North Carolina., (c) Kang Song Guan/500px prime, (b)Michael Nichols/NGC, **iv** (t) Harvard Microbiotics Lab/NGC, (c) Fox/Contributor/Getty Images, (b) U.S. Air Force photo/Lance Cheung, **2–3** [Reading for Today], used courtesy of North Carolina State University, Raleigh, North Carolina., **4** Echo/Getty Images, **6** Mark Edward Atkinson/Tracey Lee/Getty Images, **15** Monkey Business Images/Shutterstock.com, **20** Viacheslav Nikolaenko/Shutterstock.com, **21** Goucher College, **28** Shane Keyser/KRT/Newscom, **32–33** Kang Song Guan/500px prime, **34** Corbis Wire/Corbis, **36** Jiva Gupta/Corbis News/Corbis, **46** Digitalskillet/Getty Images, **48** Granger Wootz/Blend/Corbis, **52** (l) Philippe Desnerck/Getty Images, (r) Maxim Godkin/Shutterstock.com, **54** Monkey Business Images/Shutterstock.com, **63** Robert Clark/NGC, **65** ChooseMyPlate.gov/USDA, **70–71** Michael Nichols/NGC, **72** Blend Images/Ariel Skelley/The Agency Collection/Getty Images, **74** Paul Harris/Getty Images, **75** Matthieu Paley/Terra/Corbis, **83** Hero Images/Getty Images, **88** Terry Vine/Getty Images, **90** Crissy Pascual/San Diego Union-Tribune/ZUMA Press, Inc./Alamy, **99** AP Images/The Columbus Dispatch/Courtney Hergesheimer, **104–105** Harvard Microbiotics Lab/NGC, **106** Kurita Kaku/Gamma-Rapho/Getty Images, **108** Randy Olson/NGC, **117** Issei Kato/Reuters, **119** Randy Olson/NGC, **122–123** Shawn Rocco/Duke Medicine, **131** Shawn Poynter/The New York Times/Redux Pictures, **133** Mark Thiessen/National Geographic Image Collection / Alamy, **136–137** Fox/Contributor/Getty Images, **138** SSPL/Getty Images, **140** Hulton Archive/ Stringer/Getty Images, **149** Leonhard Foeger/Reuters, **154** Time Life Pictures/Getty Images, **156** Lordprice Collection/Alamy, **165** Bettmann/Corbis, **166** New York Daily News Archive/Getty Images, **170–171** U.S. Air Force photo/Lance Cheung, **172** Sarah Leen/NGC, **175** James A. Sugar/ NGC, **186** Paul Chesley/NGC, **190** Prometheus72/Shutterstock.com, **191** AP Images/Henning Kaiser/Picture-alliance/Dpa, **200** Chuck Bigger/Alamy, **202** NGM Maps/NGC, **204** Iriana Shiyan/Shutterstock.com.

NOTES

NOTES

NOTES

NOTES

NOTES

NOTES

NOTES

NOTES

NOTES

NOTES